FOR SPICESAKE

100th Anniversary Cookbook

By: MarketSpice

Editor/Photographer: Christine Hastings

Editor: Lacey Williams

Recipe Consultant: Katie Thacher

Printed in the United States of America

First Printing, 2011

ISBN 978-0-615-53605-7

MarketSpice, Inc.
14690 NE 95th Street Ste #102
Redmond, WA 98052

www.marketspice.com

Table of Contents

Introduction

MarketSpice has received many requests to publish a cookbook through the years and as we celebrate 100 years in business in 2011, we feel this monumental anniversary is the right time! Our company began its flavorful history at Seattle's historic Pike Place Market in 1911. Our flagship retail store sold bulk spices and teas in small quantities to our customers and we carry on that tradition to this day. We have created and added many new spice and tea blends since our beginning and continue to enjoy the art of product development today.

Judy Dawson, a member of the MarketSpice family for the past 30 years, commented that our method of manufacturing has not changed since she began in 1980. All tea and spice blends are still done by hand in small batches. The packaging is also done by hand, therefore, we've been happy to provide employment for many people, since we don't use machinery. Judy states "Our customers have always appreciated this aspect of our business."

As we become more educated in the importance of healthy eating, we have learned that the use of spices and herbs in cooking allows us to serve tastier dishes to our families while cutting back on fat and calories. A lean piece of chicken, fish, meat or a serving of vegetables can become appetizing and delicious when the right combination of spices is added. What is more enticing than a pot of soup, stew or chili simmering on the stove or cookies and cakes baking in the oven with the aroma of fragrant spices wafting through the air?

Nancy DeWitt, our long time Pike Place Market Retail store manager and buyer, stated she is proud to be part of a company celebrating its 100th year in business. "This position has allowed me to enjoy the loyal following of our customers. Loyal, because we have offered our customers, even in changing times, a quality product at an extraordinary value.

This is why I believe we are a Century Strong!"

Our MarketSpice staff, along with family and friends, have been very gracious in sharing recipes to contribute to this project. We have also enlisted the expertise of Katie Thacher, a local foodie from Redmond, WA who has done a tremendous job creating mouth-watering recipes just for this cookbook. We invited our customers to send in their favorite recipes using our products as well. We wholeheartedly thank everyone for helping with this endeavor.

We sincerely hope that you, our customers, will enjoy our cookbook utilizing our spices and teas, sharing our philosophy that **"Spice is the Variety of Life!"**

Symbols/Abbreviations Guide

Employee Favorite
While testing recipes for this cookbook, these dishes stood out as favorites among the MarketSpice staff.

Healthy Picks
We have designated a few choice recipes that help contribute to a healthy diet. Some individuals may have different criteria as to which foods constitute a healthy eating plan, but we chose low-fat, low sugar and low sodium options.

Spicy
Our way of giving fair warning on any recipe which includes a spicy ingredient.

Random Tip
A collection of culinary facts or recommendations not commonly known that we've compiled over our 100 years in business.

Recipe Contest Winner
Over the past year, we requested customer recipe submissions for this cookbook. After testing, these were our favorites!

lb - pound

oz – ounce

tbsp. - tablespoon

tsp. - teaspoon

SF - Salt Free

Flavorings:

(N) – All Natural

(A) – Artificial

(N&A) - Natural & Artificial

DRESSINGS, DIPS & SAUCES

Quick & Easy BBQ Sauce

Makes 3 cups

2   cups tomato sauce
½   cup apple cider or white wine vinegar
½   cup brown sugar
1   tbsp. molasses, optional
2   tsp. **Worcestershire Powder**
½   tsp. salt
2   tbsp. **Quick & Easy BBQ Sauce Blend**

1 Combine all the ingredients in a small saucepan.

2 Simmer over low heat for 20 minutes, stirring occasionally.

Serve with ribs, grilled chicken or other meat.

Creamy Herb Dressing

Makes 1 cup

½   cup mayonnaise
½   cup sour cream (substitute yogurt if desired)
1   tbsp. **Creamy Herb Dressing Mix**
2 - 4 tbsp. milk to thin

1 Combine all the ingredients, thinning with milk to the desired consistency.

2 Chill for 30 minutes.

Use to dress cucumbers or tomatoes. Serve on lettuce lined plates for decoration.

Savory Herb Vinaigrette

Makes 1½ cups

¼ cup white wine vinegar
1 cup vegetable oil
½ tsp. **Savory Herb Blend SF**
½ tsp. salt
⅛ tsp. granulated garlic
⅛ tsp. black pepper

1 Combine all of the ingredients in a jar with a tight lid.

2 Shake and allow to stand for several hours before using.

Serve with your favorite tossed salad.

Store in the refrigerator.

Spicy Bean Dip

2 tbsp. vegetable oil
⅔ cup chopped onion
¼ tsp. **Granulated Garlic**
4 tsp. **Taco Seasoning SF**
1 8oz can tomato sauce
¼ tsp. salt or more to taste
⅛ tsp. pepper
1 lb can refried beans

1 Heat the oil in a medium saucepan. Add the onion and sauté until tender.

2 Add the **Granulated Garlic** and **Taco Seasoning SF** and cook, stirring continuously for about 1 minute.

3 Add the tomato sauce, salt, pepper and simmer for 2 - 3 minutes.

4 Allow to cool slightly and then add the refried beans, stirring until completely blended.

Serve at room temperature with tortilla chips for dipping.

Vegetable Chip Dip

Makes 2 cups

1 cup mayonnaise
1 cup sour cream
2 tbsp. **Veggie Chip Dip Mix** (add more
   to taste)

1 Combine all ingredients in a medium mixing bowl and stir well.

2 Refrigerate for one hour to blend flavors.

Serve with vegetables, chips or crackers.

Texas BBQ Sauce

Makes 2½ cups

1 6oz can tomato paste
½ cup butter
½ cup apple cider vinegar
½ cup ketchup or 1 can diced tomatoes
¾ cup water
2 tbsp. molasses
2 tbsp. lemon juice
2 tbsp. **Worcestershire Powder**
1 small onion, minced
½ tsp. salt
2 tbsp. **Texas BBQ Sauce Blend**

1 Melt the butter in a small saucepan.

2 Add the onion and sauté until translucent, about 3 minutes.

3 Add the other ingredients all at once and stir well.

4 Simmer for 20 to 30 minutes if using ketchup and one hour if using canned tomatoes.

5 Puree the mixture in the blender to achieve a smooth sauce.

Vegetable Chip Dip

Dressings, Dips & Sauces

Beaumonde Grilling Sauce

½ tsp. **Beaumonde**

½ cup melted butter

1 tsp. lemon juice

1 Combine all of the ingredients in a bowl .

2 Use to baste meats while grilling or baking.

Garlic Herb Cheese Spread

8 oz cream cheese, softened

2 cloves minced garlic (or ½ tsp. granulated garlic)

1 tsp. **Savory Herb Blend SF**

¼ tsp. salt or more to taste

Milk to thin if desired

1 Combine the cream cheese, garlic, **Savory Herb Blend SF** and salt together in a medium mixing bowl and stir well.

2 Add milk to thin if desired. Put into a covered container and chill before serving.

Serve with crackers.

Random Tip#1

Herb & Spice Storage: Store in a cool, dark place.
Humidity, light and heat will cause herbs & spices
to lose their flavor more quickly.

Bleu Cheese Dressing

1 cup sour cream

1 ½ tbsp. vinegar

2 tbsp. mayonnaise

1 tbsp. parsley flakes

2 tbsp. **Bleu Cheese Herb Dressing Mix**

¼ cup bleu cheese (more if desired)

1 In a small mixing bowl combine the sour cream, vinegar, mayonnaise, parsley and **Bleu Cheese Herb Dressing Mix** and blend together well.

2 Stir in the bleu cheese and mix well.

3 Let stand for at least 1 hour before serving.

Serve with salads, eggs, mixed vegetables or potatoes.

Buttermilk Herb Dressing

1 tbsp. **Buttermilk Herb Dressing Mix**

1 cup buttermilk

1 cup mayonnaise

1 In a small mixing bowl combine all ingredients and blend well.

2 Refrigerate for several hours before serving.

Serve with fresh vegetables and salads.

Tuscan White Bean & Artichoke Dip

Tuscan White Bean & Artichoke Dip

Makes about 2 cups

1   can cannellini or other white beans
1   small jar artichoke hearts
2   tbsp. **Veggie Chip Dip Mix**
1   clove fresh garlic or 2 tbsp. roasted
    garlic paste
¼   cup olive oil

1 Place all ingredients in a food processor and pulse until the dip becomes smooth and thick.

2 Scrape into a bowl and serve with pita chips or toasted baguette.

Green Magic Dressing

½   cup mayonnaise
½   cup sour cream
2 ½ tbsp. lemon juice
4   tbsp. milk to thin to desired consistency
½   tsp. **Granulated Garlic**
¼   tsp. **Ground White Pepper**
4   tsp. **Green Magic Dressing Mix**

1 In a medium mixing bowl combine all ingredients and blend well.

2 Chill for at least 1 hour before serving.

This dressing is excellent for mixed green salads or cold vegetables.

MarketSpice Cranberry Glaze

2 cups **MarketSpice Cinnamon-Orange Black Tea**, brewed

4 tsp. corn starch

4 tbsp. cranberry sauce (jellied or regular)

1 tbsp. brown sugar

1 In a medium size mixing bowl stir corn starch into tea until dissolved.

2 Put in a medium size saucepan and add the cranberry sauce (smash with fork first-if using jellied) and brown sugar.

3 Bring just to a boil and simmer until slightly thickened. There will still be pieces of cranberry jelly.

Serve as a sauce over turkey, chicken or pork as a lighter, sweeter alternative to gravy. Use as a glaze over pork roast or chicken the last 20 minutes of baking.

Parmesan Dressing

1 ⅓ cups vegetable oil

⅓ cup white wine vinegar

¼ cup grated Parmigiano-Reggiano cheese

3 tbsp. **Parmesan Dressing Mix**

1 ½ tbsp. **Italian Vinaigrette Dressing Mix**

1 In a small mixing bowl combine all ingredients and whisk vigorously to blend well.

2 Chill for at least one hour before serving.

Random Tip#2

Seasonings: Use a light hand when seasoning with herbs & spices. The goal is to complement the dish without overwhelming the flavor of the food. You can always add more as needed.

Italian Vinaigrette

1 cup vegetable oil or olive oil

⅓ cup white wine vinegar

1 tbsp. parsley flakes

2 tbsp. lemon juice

1 ½ tbsp. **Italian Vinaigrette Dressing Mix**

1 In a small mixing bowl combine all ingredients and whisk vigorously to blend well.

2 Chill for at least one hour before serving.

Serve with vegetables, salads, meats or fish.

Fettuccini Sauce

1 tbsp. olive oil

4 cloves garlic, finely chopped

1 small onion, finely chopped

2 cans (28oz each) whole Italian style tomatoes, drained

4 tsp. **Fettuccini Spice Blend**

½ tsp. salt

½ tsp. pepper

1 Heat oil in a medium size saucepan on medium heat.

2 Cook garlic and onion in oil until tender.

3 Place tomatoes in blender or food processor and process until smooth (or chop finely by hand).

4 Stir tomatoes, **Fettuccini Spice Blend**, salt and pepper into the sauce pan.

5 Heat sauce to boiling. Reduce heat and simmer uncovered for 45 minutes, stirring occasionally.

Add this sauce to your favorite type of pasta and add a little parmesan cheese if desired.

Dressings, Dips & Sauces

Sunshine Dip

Makes 2 cups

1 cup sour cream
1 cup mayonnaise
4 tbsp. **Country Herb Blend** (or SF)

1 Combine all of the ingredients in a medium mixing bowl and blend well.

2 Refrigerate for at least one hour before serving to blend flavors.

Serve with crackers, chips or vegetables. Thin with milk for use as a dressing on salads.

Piquant French Dressing

1 ¼ cup vegetable oil
½ cup vinegar
2 tsp. sugar (optional)
1 tbsp. **French Salad Dressing Mix**

1 In a small mixing bowl combine all ingredients and whisk vigorously to blend well.

2 Chill for at least one hour before serving.

If separation occurs whisk again to blend and toss with your favorite salad greens.

Sunshine Dip

Dressings, Dips & Sauces

Marinara Sauce

Makes 8 cups

3 tbsp. olive oil
2 onions, finely diced
2 large (28oz) cans crushed tomatoes
1 small can tomato paste
1 tbsp. sugar
½ tsp. salt, to taste
½ cup full bodied red wine, optional
2 tbsp. **Marinara Blend**
¼ cup finely chopped fresh parsley
½ cup grated parmesan cheese, optional

1 Heat the olive oil in a large saucepan. Add the onion to the pan and sauté until browned but not burnt (8 minutes).

2 Add the crushed tomatoes, tomato paste, sugar, salt, **Marinara Blend,** red wine, (optional) and bring to a simmer.

3 Maintain a simmer for at least 20 minutes and up to an hour.

4 Add the chopped parsley and parmesan if using and stir to combine.

Serve with any type of pasta, baked chicken breasts, as part of pizza, etc.

Ranchero Salsa Dip

Makes 2 cups

1 8oz can tomato sauce
1 large tomato, finely chopped
1 tbsp. lemon juice
½ cup sliced black olives
2 ½ tbsp. **Ranchero Mix**

1 Combine all ingredients in a medium mixing bowl.

2 Cover and refrigerate for several hours or overnight to blend flavors.

Serve with crackers, tortilla chips or with eggs.

Honey Mustard Dressing

Makes 1¼ cups

½ cup sugar

⅓ cup honey

¼ cup lemon juice

2 tbsp. **Honey Mustard Dressing Mix**

¾ cup oil

1 Combine all ingredients in a medium mixing bowl.

2 Cover and refrigerate for several hours or overnight to blend flavors.

Serve with your favorite salad greens. Keeps well in refrigerator for several weeks.

Spicy BBQ Sauce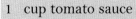

1   cup tomato sauce

1   6oz can tomato paste

1   cup water

2   tbsp. butter

1   tbsp. **Worcestershire Powder**

1   tbsp. vinegar

½   tsp. salt (if desired)

2   tbsp. **Spicy BBQ Sauce Blend**

1 Combine all ingredients and simmer uncovered for 1 hour or more, stirring occasionally.

Serve with your favorite BBQ or grilled meat.

Random Tip#3

Barbecuing: Whenever barbecuing, use tongs to turn the meat. Forks should not be used as the punch holes in the flesh and allow the natural juices to escape. This can allow the meat to lose flavor and become chewy.

APPETIZERS

Smoked Hummus

Smoked Hummus 🍎

1 can chickpeas (garbanzo beans)
2 tbsp. tahini
   Juice and zest of ½ a lemon
½ cup olive oil
1 tsp. **Paprika, Smoked**
   Garnish: olive oil

1 In a food processor blend the chickpeas, tahini, lemon juice and lemon zest until mostly smooth.

2 With the food processor running, add the olive oil in a steady stream. Blend until smooth.

Serve in a bowl, pour a bit of olive oil over the hummus and dust with **Paprika, Smoked**.

Zesty Salsa 🌶️

2 tbsp. extra virgin olive oil
½ cup chopped onion
¼ cup chopped green pepper
1 16oz can tomatoes
1 8oz can tomato sauce
1 tbsp. **Taco Seasoning SF**
½ tsp. **Granulated Garlic**

1 Heat olive oil over medium heat in a medium size pan. Add the onion and green pepper and sauté until onion is soft.

2 Coarsely puree the tomatoes in a food processor or blender and add to the pan with the tomato sauce, **Taco Seasoning SF** and **Granulated Garlic**.

3 Stir all ingredients together until well blended.

4 Reduce heat to low and simmer for 15 minutes.

Serve with any food that would benefit from a zesty sauce such as tacos, nachos, omelets, meats and burgers.

Chickpea Cocktail Snacks

2 tbsp. olive oil

1 15oz can chickpeas (garbanzo beans), drained, rinsed and dried

1 tbsp. **Market Seasoning w/ Salt** or **Market Seasoning Natural w/ Salt**

1 tbsp. sherry vinegar

1 Heat the olive oil in a frying pan over high heat. When the oil is hot, add the chickpeas and stir for 3 to 5 minutes or until they begin to darken in color (they may pop some while cooking, so a splatter screen can be helpful).

2 Remove from heat and stir in the **Market Seasoning** and vinegar. Serve.

Random Tip#4

Cooking Spices: For dishes that cook for a long period of time, add spices and herbs an hour or less before serving. Cooking spices for too long may result in overly strong flavors.

Herbed Cucumber Finger Sandwiches

½ tbsp. **Savory Herb Blend SF**

8 oz whipped cream cheese, room
temperature

1 English cucumber

1 loaf sliced white bread

1 Stir the **Savory Herb Blend SF** into the cream cheese. Set aside for about 20 minutes to allow the flavors to meld.

2 Thinly slice the cucumber. There is no need to peel or seed it if you use an English cucumber.

3 Remove the crusts from the bread. Thinly spread cream cheese on the whole surface. Cut each slice into quarters. Top two of the pieces of bread with a cucumber slice and place remaining two pieces of bread on top to create a sandwich.

Use toothpicks to hold them together if you like.

Appetizers

Jamaican Jerk Chicken Wings

Serves 4 – 6

2   lbs chicken wings
3   tbsp. **Jamaican Jerk Seasoning**
2   tbsp. soy sauce
1   small onion, finely chopped (or blended to
    a paste in a food processor)
2   tbsp. vegetable oil
1   tbsp. molasses
2   tbsp. Dijon mustard
1   tsp. salt

1 Cut the wing tips off the chicken wings and then cut the wings in half at the joint.

2 In a large mixing bowl, combine the **Jamaican Jerk Seasoning**, soy sauce, onion, oil, molasses, mustard and salt.

3 Add the chicken wings to the bowl and toss to thoroughly coat with the marinade. Cover with plastic wrap and refrigerate for at least 3 hours or preferably overnight.

4 Preheat your oven's broiler. Lightly oil the rack of a broiler pan using cooking spray or vegetable oil and arrange the wings on the rack.

5 Broil the wings (they should be about 4 inches from the heat source) for 8 to 10 minutes or until they are golden brown.

6 Remove the pan from the oven, turn the wings and continue to broil until both sides are browned and the meat is cooked through (approximately 4 minutes).

Serve hot.

Italian Herb Cheese Puffs

Makes about 40 small puffs

½ cup water
4 tbsp. unsalted butter
¼ tsp. salt
½ cup flour
3 eggs
⅔ cup grated sharp cheddar
1 tbsp. **Ground Italian Seasoning**

1 Preheat the oven to 400°F. Line a baking sheet with parchment paper.

2 In a small saucepan, bring the water, butter and salt to a boil. Add the flour all at once and whisk rapidly until it comes together in a ball.

3 Remove the pan from the heat and add the eggs, one at a time, whisking between each addition.

4 Add the cheese and **Ground Italian Seasoning**, and whisk together.

5 Spoon the dough into small mounds (about ½ tablespoons each) on the baking sheet.

6 Bake for 20 minutes or until golden.

Serve warm from the oven.

Random Tip#5
Dried Herbs: Do not use dried herbs in the same
quantity as fresh. Use ⅓ the amount in dried as is
called for fresh.

Curried Samosas

Part 1 - Dough:
Makes 20 small samosas

1 cup all-purpose flour
½ cup whole wheat flour
1 tsp. salt
4 tbsp. oil
6 tbsp. water

1 In a food processor, process the flours and salt to mix. Add the oil and process until the mixture resembles cornmeal in texture.

2 Add the water and process for 1 minute. Remove the dough to a cutting board. Form into a ball and rub with a little oil. Let rest, covered in plastic wrap for 30 minutes.

Make the filling.

Part 2 - Filling:

1 tbsp. vegetable oil
1 small onion, diced
2 pounds potatoes, preferably purple potatoes, cooked and diced
1 cup fresh or frozen peas
3 tbsp. **Curry Powder, Madras**
2 tbsp. chopped cilantro, optional
  Oil for frying

1 Heat the oil over medium heat. Add the onion and cook until soft.

2 Add the potatoes, peas and **Curry Powder, Madras**. Cook over low heat for 3 minutes or until heated.

Stir in cilantro if using.

1 After dough has rested, knead for a minute or two, and then divide into 10 equal balls.

2 Take one ball, flatten it and roll it to 5 inches in diameter.

3 Using water around the edges to help it stick together, form the circle into a cone. Stuff with filling and close over the top, using water to seal it.

4 Heat 2 inches of oil to 375° in a deep pan. Fry samosas in batches of 4 or 5, for about 3 minutes each or until golden brown.

Serve warm.

Variation: For healthier version, instead of frying, brush each samosa with egg yolk and bake on a cookie sheet in a 400°oven for 10 minutes.

Appetizers

Smoked Salmon Deviled Eggs

1 Place the eggs in a pot large enough to hold them all in one layer and cover with cold water. Bring to a full boil, cover, remove from heat and let sit for 20 minutes.

2 Drain and cover with cold water.

3 When cool, peel the eggs, slice them in half lengthwise and remove the yolks, reserving them for the filling.

Makes 20 deviled eggs

10 eggs
½ cup sour cream (NOT nonfat or lowfat)
1 heaping tbsp. **Veggie Chip Dip Mix**
2 ½ oz smoked salmon, flaked (choose drier "hot-smoked" salmon as opposed to lox-like "cold-smoked")
½ tsp. **Paprika, Smoked**

4 With an electric mixer, beat the egg yolks with the sour cream and **Veggie Chip Dip Mix** until mostly smooth (some small lumps are fine).

5 Mix in the smoked salmon and stir until no large chunks remain. Fill each egg with this mixture and dust with **Paprika, Smoked**.

Let rest for at least 10 minutes before serving to allow the spices to blend.

Random Tip#6
Boiling Eggs: Add a pinch of salt to the water to keep shells from cracking.

Pickled Vegetables

Makes 4 cups

1   quart plus 1 cup water
3   tbsp. salt
4   cups mixed vegetables (try any mixture of
    sugar snap peas, green beans, asparagus,
    carrots, red bell peppers, cucumbers,
    onions, beets and even rhubarb)
½   cup sugar
1   cup white vinegar
¼   cup **Pickling Spice**

1 In a small saucepan, heat the first quart of water with the salt until the salt dissolves.

2 Place the vegetables in this brine and let soak for 4 hours. Drain the vegetables, discarding the brine.

3 In another small saucepan, bring the last cup of water to a boil and add the sugar, vinegar and **Pickling Spice**. Remove from the heat and stir to dissolve the sugar. Let this mixture cool for a few minutes.

4 Place the vegetables in a large container and pour the vinegar mixture over them.

5 Cover, cool and refrigerate for at least 12 hours before serving. This will keep for a week in the refrigerator.

Party Guacamole ✨

¼ red onion, finely diced
2 tbsp. freshly squeezed lime juice
2 tbsp. **Salsa Mix**
2 avocados
1 small tomato, finely diced
2 tbsp. chopped cilantro (add more to taste)

1 In a medium bowl, combine the red onion, lime juice and **Salsa Mix**. Let sit for 15 minutes to allow the onions to mellow.

2 Add the avocados and tomato. With two forks, squish the avocado into a guacamole while mixing it with the other ingredients. Stir in the cilantro.

Serve with tortilla chips or on your favorite taco or quesadilla. Add ½ cup sour cream for creamier guacamole.

Greek Spinach & Feta Tarts

Makes 45 small tarts

1 tbsp. extra-virgin olive oil
1 onion, chopped
10 – 12 oz spinach, washed
3 tbsp. water
4 eggs
¼ tsp. salt
¼ tsp. ground pepper
8 oz crumbled feta cheese
3 tbsp. bread crumbs
1 tbsp. **Greek Seasoning**
⅓ cup roasted pine nuts
3 packages phyllo tart shells

1 Preheat oven to 375°F. Heat the olive oil in a large saucepan over medium heat. Add the onion and sauté until it begins to brown.

2 Add the spinach and water and stir until the spinach wilts down. Remove from heat and squeeze the excess water from the spinach.

3 In a food processor, combine the spinach mixture, eggs, salt, pepper, feta, bread crumbs and **Greek Seasoning**. Pulse a few times to finely chop and combine; mixture should not be completely smooth. Mix the pine nuts in by hand.

4 Line a baking sheet with parchment paper and place the empty tart shells on it. Fill each one to slightly overflowing with the spinach filling.

5 Bake for about 15 minutes or until the filling is set and the phyllo begins to brown.

Appetizers

SOUPS & CHILIES

Bombay Curried Carrot Soup 🍎

Serves 6 - 8

3   tbsp. extra virgin olive oil
1   medium onion, coarsely chopped
2   celery stalks, sliced
1 ½ lbs carrots, peeled and sliced ½ inch thick
1 - 2 tbsp. **Bombay Mix**, to taste
3   cups low sodium chicken broth
3   cups carrot juice (or your favorite vegetable juice)
    Salt to taste

1 Heat the olive oil in a large saucepan over medium-high heat.

2 Add the onion, celery and carrots to the pan. Sauté for about 8 minutes or until the vegetables begin to caramelize.

3 Stir in the **Bombay Mix**, chicken broth and carrot juice. Bring to a simmer and reduce the heat to low. Simmer for 20 minutes, or until the carrots are very soft.

4 Transfer the mixture in batches to a blender or food processor (a blender will produce a smoother soup) and puree until smooth.

Add additional chicken broth if necessary to thin, season with salt if desired and serve.

Three Meat Chili

Recipe Contest Winner!
John from Enumclaw, WA

Serves 8+

2 tbsp. olive oil

2 lbs. sirloin steak, cut into 1 inch cubes

½ lb ground beef

1 12oz chorizo sausage, casing removed, cut into ½ inch cubes

1 large onion, chopped

¼ cup **Chili Powder, Regular**

1 tbsp. **Garlic Salt**

2 tsp. **Ground Cumin**

1 tsp. **Whole Basil**

3 ½ cups beef broth

2 15oz cans whole tomatoes, drained

1 cup cilantro, chopped

1 **6" Cinnamon Stick**

3 **Whole Bay Leaves**

2 green jalapenos, slit lengthwise 3 times each

1 tbsp. yellow cornmeal

Salt and pepper to taste

Shredded cheese

Sour cream

1 Place oil in a large, heavy pot over medium heat. Brown the sirloin in batches.

2 Remove to a bowl.

3 Add ground beef, chorizo and onions to the pot and brown. Make sure to break up the meat. Drain out the fat.

4 Return sirloin to the pot.

5 Stir in the remaining ingredients except for the cheese and sour cream.

6 Bring to a boil, reduce heat and simmer for 2 hours. Stir occasionally, breaking up tomatoes.

7 Before serving discard cinnamon stick, bay leaves and jalapenos.

Serve with shredded cheese and/or sour cream.

Random Tip#7
Kitchen Shears: A simple way to sharpen kitchen shears is cutting into a piece of steel wool.

Albondigas Soup

Recipe Contest Winner!
Angie from El Centro, CA

Serves 8

4 tbsp. **Beef Soup Base**
2 medium onions, peeled and chopped
2 tbsp. **Minced Garlic**
1 cup chopped celery
3 lbs lean ground beef
1 cup uncooked white long grain rice
2 eggs
3 tbsp. **Mexicali Mix**
1 lb baby carrots
6 potatoes, cut into ½ inch cubes
5 grey Mexican squash or zucchini, sliced thick
  Salt and pepper to taste

1 In a deep soup pot, combine **Beef Soup Base** with 4 quarts of water and bring to a simmer.

2 Add onions, **Minced Garlic** and celery and bring to a boil

3 Meanwhile in a large mixing bowl, combine ground beef, rice, eggs, 1 tablespoon of the **Mexicali Mix** and pepper to taste.

4 Form into small meatballs and drop individually into boiling broth.

5 Add potatoes, carrots, the remaining 2 tablespoons of **Mexicali Mix** and continue boiling gently for 30 minutes.

6 Turn heat to low and simmer, add tomatoes and squash and cook until squash is tender.

Serve with Spanish rice and lemon wedges.

Green Chili Stew

1 Heat oil in a large pot over high heat and brown the meat in batches. Remove meat to a plate and set aside.

2 In the same oil sauté onions until golden brown. Add **Minced Garlic** and sauté for 1 minute. Return meat to the pot along with any juices that may have accumulated.

3 Add the broth, potatoes and salt and bring to a boil. Reduce heat and simmer for 1 hour or until potatoes are tender.

4 Add the green chili and red bell pepper and cook for an additional 15 to 20 minutes.

Add **Cilantro**, stir and serve.

Serves 6

3	tbsp. vegetable oil
1 ½	lbs beef sirloin, cut into 1 inch pieces
1	small onion, diced
1	tbsp. **Minced Garlic**
6	cups chicken broth
1	lb red or white potatoes cut into ½ inch cubes
1	tsp. salt
3	cups roasted, peeled, chopped green chili or freeze dried green chili
½	small red pepper, diced
2	tbsp. **Cilantro**

Soups & Chilies

Mexicali Tortilla Soup

Part 1 - Soup:

1 tbsp. vegetable oil
1 onion, chopped
1 ½ cup shredded cooked chicken
2 tbsp. **Mexicali Mix**
6 cups chicken broth
1 can finely diced tomatoes
1 tbsp. tomato paste
½ can black beans
½ can corn
1 small can green chilies, chopped
    Salt to taste

Part 2 - Toppings:

½ cup coarsely chopped cilantro
2 green onions, white and green parts, thinly sliced
1 large or 2 small avocados, sliced
1 lime, sliced into 6 wedges
¾ cup Monterey Jack cheese
    Homemade tortilla chips (see page 120)
    or 1 cup crushed tortilla chips

1 Heat the oil in a large saucepan over medium-high heat.

2 Add the onion and sauté until it begins to brown. Add the chicken and the **Mexicali Mix**. Cook for about 1 minute.

3 Add the rest of the soup ingredients, bring to a low boil and reduce heat to medium-low. Cook at a simmer for 20 minutes. Taste and season with salt.

1 Place the topping ingredients in small bowls or plates.

2 Allow guests to add toppings as desired.

Random Tip#8
Soup: If you over-salt a pot of soup, drop in a peeled potato to absorb the excess. Remember to remove potato before serving.

Pictured with Homemade Tortilla Chips, 120

Soups & Chilies

Coconut Chicken Curry

Bloody Mary Red Pepper Soup

Serves 4 - 6

3   tbsp. olive oil
1   small sweet onion, finely chopped
4   red bell peppers, stems cut off and seeds removed, diced
1   tbsp. **Bloody Mary Mix** plus additional as needed
2   tbsp. flour
4   cups chicken broth
1   tbsp. tomato paste
¼   cup heavy cream, optional
    Salt, as needed

1 Heat the olive oil in a large saucepan over medium heat. Add the onions and red peppers, reduce the heat to medium-low and sauté for 8 minutes.

2 Add the **Bloody Mary Mix** and flour, and continue to sauté for another 10 minutes.

3 Whisk in the chicken stock and tomato paste. Raise heat to high until the soup begins to boil, then reduce to medium-low and simmer for 30 to 45 minutes.

4 Puree in a blender. A food processor works too but the soup will not be quite as smooth. For an extremely smooth soup, pass it through a strainer as well.

5 Return to the pan. Stir in the cream, if using and simmer for 10 more minutes. Taste and add additional salt and **Bloody Mary Mix** as needed.

Coconut Chicken Curry

Serves 6

1   tbsp. vegetable oil or ghee
1   large onion, finely diced
2   tbsp. **Curry Powder, Chicken**
1   can coconut milk
4   cups chicken broth
1   cup cooked chicken, shredded
½   cup long grain white rice

1 Heat the oil in a medium saucepan over medium-high heat. When the oil is hot, add the onion and sauté until it begins to brown.

2 Add the **Curry Powder, Chicken** and stir. Add the coconut milk to the pan and return to a simmer.

3 Add the chicken broth, rice and cooked chicken. Bring the soup to a simmer and cook for 20 minutes or until the rice is fully cooked. Serve hot.

Beef & Bitter Chocolate Chili

1 Season the beef cubes with the salt and pepper.

2 Heat the olive oil in a large saucepan over high heat. When the oil is hot but not smoking, add the beef in a single layer (if possible) and let cook undisturbed for 1 or 2 minutes or until one side is nicely browned. Turn the meat and brown the other side for 1 minute. Stir for another minute to brown the other sides.

3 Remove the beef from the pan to a plate and cover with foil. If you couldn't fit all the meat in the first time, add a little more oil and repeat with the rest of the meat. Remove it to the same plate and cover.

4 When you have finished browning the meat, add the onions to the pan and reduce heat to medium-high. Sauté the onions until they begin to brown, about 5 to 7 minutes.

5 Add the **Chili Powder, Hot** and the tomato paste, stir to combine and sauté for an additional 2 minutes. Return the beef to the pan.

Serves 6

2	tbsp. salt
1	tbsp. freshly ground pepper
2	tbsp. olive oil
3	lbs stewing beef, cut into cubes (shoulder or bottom round work well)
2	medium onions, diced
¼	cup **Chili Powder, Hot** (substitute **Chili Powder, Mild** if desired)
2	tbsp. tomato paste
1	28oz can diced tomatoes with their juices
1	can kidney beans
1	can cannelloni or other white beans
1	cup red wine
	Additional water
2	tbsp. grated unsweetened chocolate
2	cups shredded white cheddar

6 Add the tomatoes, kidney beans, white beans and red wine. Add additional water if needed to almost cover the beef with liquid. Bring the chili mixture to a boil, add the grated chocolate, stir and reduce the heat to medium-low. Cover and simmer for 2 hours.

Taste and add additional salt if needed. Serve with the grated cheddar cheese.

Random Tip#9
Green Tea: When using broth or cooking vegetables, replace 1 cup of liquid with 1 cup of brewed green tea. You'll get the benefits of green tea in your dish as well as adding a more interesting flavor.

Soups & Chilies

Pumpkin & Coconut Seafood Bisque

Serves 6

1   large can pumpkin puree (make sure it is not spiced or seasoned)

1   can coconut milk

2   cups clam broth (or substitute chicken broth)

2   tbsp. **<u>Chili Lime Rub</u>**

1   lb mussels

½   lb large shrimp, peeled and deveined

½   lb lobster tail meat, optional
     Cilantro, for garnish

1 In a large saucepan, combine the pumpkin puree, coconut milk, clam or chicken broth and **<u>Chili Lime Rub</u>**. Bring to a simmer and cook for 20 minutes.

2 Add the shrimp and mussels (and lobster if using), return to a low boil and cover. Cook until the mussels are open and the shrimp is pink and begins to curl, about 5 minutes.

Spoon into bowls and top with cilantro, if desired.

Chicken Posole 🎀

Recipe Contest Winner!
Angie from El Centro, CA

Serves 8

10 chicken thighs with bones and skins
1   large onion, peeled and chopped
2   tbsp. **Minced Garlic**
2   tbsp. **Mexicali Mix**
    Salt and pepper to taste
1   108oz can white hominy (not Mexican
    style), drained and rinsed (#10 can)
1   quart chicken broth
1   7oz can chopped green chilies
1   4oz can chopped green chilies
    Chopped cabbage
    Lemon wedges

1 Rinse chicken thighs under cold water and place in a large soup pot.

2 Cover with water, add onion and **Minced Garlic** and boil for 1 hour.

3 Turn heat to low and simmer gently. Remove chicken from pot and allow to cool.

4 Remove skin and bones and return chicken meat to pot.

5 Add hominy, large can of chilies, **Mexicali Mix** and salt and pepper to taste.

6 Return to boil, reduce to medium-low and continue to cook for 1 hour, stirring and adding chicken broth occasionally.

7 Add small can of chilies before serving.

Serve with chopped cabbage and lemon wedges.

Moroccan Two Lentil Soup

Serves 8

1   tbsp. olive oil
1   medium yellow onion, diced
1 ½ cups pink lentils
½   cup lentils de Puy or other French-style
    Lentils*
1   tbsp. **Ras el Hanout**
6   cups chicken broth
½   medium carrot, finely grated
    Zest of ½ orange
    Juice of 1 small orange
    Scant ¼ cup peanut butter, optional
1 - 2 cups water, as needed

1 Heat the olive oil in a deep soup pot. Once the oil is hot, add the onion and stir until it softens but does not brown.

2 Add both types of lentils and the **Ras el Hanout** and stir for one minute.

3 Add the chicken broth, carrot, orange juice, orange zest and peanut butter (optional). Bring to a gentle simmer, cover and let simmer for at least 45 minutes.

4 Whisk the soup to bring the pink lentils to a coarse puree, while allowing the French lentils to keep their shape. Add enough water to bring the soup to the desired thickness. Serve hot.

*If you have trouble finding these particular lentils, you can substitute using whatever lentils are available in your local market.

Random Tip#10
Browning Onions: Add a little milk to onions while frying as this helps to retain the rich color and keeps onions from burning.

Soups & Chilies

Cucumber Melon Gazpacho

Serves 6

1 ripe 4 to 5 pound cantaloupe, peeled and cut into 1 inch cubes

1 cucumber, peeled and sliced into 1 inch segments

1 small tomato, coarsely diced

2 slices white sandwich bread, crusts removed

¼ cup extra virgin olive oil

2 tbsp. sherry vinegar

½ tsp. **Jalapeno Powder**

Zest of 1 lime

Ice water

2 oz Italian or high quality domestic prosciutto, sliced into 1 inch by ¼ inch slices

1 In a medium bowl, soak the sandwich bread in enough water to fully submerge it for 10 minutes. Drain the bread and squeeze out some of the water.

2 In a blender or food processor, blend the soaked bread, cantaloupe, cucumber, tomato, olive oil, vinegar and **Jalapeno Powder** until completely smooth, about 1 minute.

3 Add additional ice water to thin the soup to your desired consistency. Chill in the refrigerator for at least 45 minutes and up to a day.

Serve in chilled bowls, topping each bowl with a few slices of prosciutto and a pinch of lime zest.

 Taco Soup **Recipe Contest Winner!**
Diana from Bothell, WA

1 lb ground beef

1 small onion, chopped

1 tsp. salt

1 tsp. pepper

1 15oz can pinto beans, rinsed and drained

1 15oz can black beans, rinsed and drained

1 15oz can kidney beans, rinsed and drained

2 16oz cans stewed tomatoes, cut into smaller pieces

3 - 4 tbsp. **Taco Seasoning SF**

3 - 4 tbsp. **Buttermilk Herb Dressing Mix**

1 ½ cups water

Shredded cheese

Sour cream

Tortilla chips

1 In a large skillet brown the beef and drain out the fat.

2 Transfer to a large pot and add all other ingredients except the cheese, sour cream and tortilla chips.

3 Bring to a boil, turn down heat to low and simmer for 30 minutes.

Top with cheese and/or sour cream. Serve with tortilla chips and/or cornbread.

Random Tip#11

Beef Patties: Use a gentle touch when shaping ground beef patties. Over handling will result in a firm, compact texture after cooking. Don't press or flatten with spatula during cooking.

Soups & Chilies

ENTREES

Spiced Pecan Waffles with Caramelized Bananas ✦

Part 1 - Waffles:

2   eggs
2   cups all-purpose flour
1 ¾ cups milk
½   cup melted butter
1   tbsp. sugar
4   tsp. baking powder
¼   tsp. salt
2   tsp. **Sweet Baking Spice**
½   cup pecans, chopped

1 Preheat the waffle iron. In a large bowl, beat the eggs with a hand beater until they become fluffy.

2 Add the flour, milk, butter, sugar, baking powder, salt and **Sweet Baking Spice**. Beat just until smooth. Stir in the chopped pecans.

3 Spray preheated waffle iron with non-stick cooking spray. Cook the waffles according to the manufacturer's instructions.

Serve hot with a spoonful of caramelized bananas.

Part 2 - Bananas:

3   tbsp. butter
½   cup **Brown Sugar**
3   bananas, sliced
½   tsp. **Vanilla Powder**

1 In a medium skillet, heat the butter until melted.

2 Stir in the **Brown Sugar**.

3 Add the bananas and cook for about 4 minutes or until cooked and syrupy. Stir in the **Vanilla Powder**.

Random Tip#12
Homemade Whipping Cream: Put the bowl and egg beater in the fridge to chill down before adding the cream and whipping. The cream will thicken much faster.

Sausage & Egg Frittata

Serves 6

½ lb ground pork (not lean pork; this recipe needs the fat)

2 tbsp. **Sausage Mix**

8 eggs

¼ tsp. salt

1 cup grated cheese (such as Cheddar, Mozzarella or Monterey Jack)

2 tbsp. olive oil

1 green pepper, diced

1 small onion, diced

2 tbsp. butter

1 Preheat the oven to 350°F.

2 In a small mixing bowl, use your hands to mix the ground pork with the **Sausage Mix**.

3 In a medium mixing bowl, beat the eggs with the salt and cheese. Set aside.

4 Heat the oil in a nonstick oven-safe 10-inch skillet over medium-low heat. Add the pork in an even layer and allow to brown on one side for 1 to 2 minutes. With a spatula, break up the pork and sauté for an additional 3 or 4 minutes or until cooked through. Remove the pork to a mixing bowl.

5 Add the pepper and the onion to the pan and sauté for about 6 minutes or until they are soft but not too browned. Remove the veggies to the bowl with the pork and mix the two together.

6 Swirl the butter into the pan until it is fully melted. Add half the eggs, evenly add the pork and vegetable mixture and cover with the other half of the egg mixture. Without disturbing, let the frittata cook on the stovetop for 3 minutes or until the edges begin to set.

7 Transfer the skillet to the oven and cook for another 12 minutes or until the center is set. Remove from the oven, slice into wedges and serve. For a little extra flavor add salsa and/or sour cream.

Smoked Salmon & Spinach Quiche

Serves 8

3   oz fresh spinach, stems and tough parts
    removed
1   tbsp. olive oil
6   eggs
1 ½ cups whole milk
½   tsp. salt
¼   tsp. freshly ground pepper
1   tbsp. **Seafood Seasoning**
4   oz smoked salmon, flaked
1   premade 9-inch pie crust

1 Preheat your oven to 375°F.

2 Wash but do not dry the spinach. Heat the oil in a large saucepan over medium-high heat.

3 Add the wet spinach and stir for about 2 minutes. Cover and allow to steam for about 5 minutes or until completely wilted. Remove the lid and sauté the spinach another minute. Transfer the cooked spinach to a strainer and press out any remaining liquid. When it is cool enough to handle, transfer the spinach to a cutting board and chop it into small bits.

4 In a large bowl beat together the eggs, milk, salt, pepper and **Seafood Seasoning**. Add the cooked spinach and the salmon, and stir to combine.

5 Pour the mixture into the pie crust and bake for 35 minutes, or until the quiche is set in the middle and browned on top.

Cool on a wire rack for at least 5 minutes before cutting into wedges and serving.

Random Tip#13

Omelets: Add 1 tablespoon of water to an egg before beating for a more fluffy, larger omelet.

MarketSpice Tea Oatmeal

1 cup boiling water

1 tbsp. **MarketSpice Cinnamon-Orange Black Tea** leaves

½ cup oatmeal

1 tbsp. **Brown Sugar** or more to taste

2 tbsp. **Strawberry Pieces**

1 Boil water, add **MarketSpice Cinnamon-Orange Black Tea** and steep for 3 to 5 minutes or longer if a stronger taste is desired. Strain tea into microwave-safe bowl.

2 Add dry oatmeal and microwave per oatmeal instructions.

3 Top cooked oatmeal with **Brown Sugar** and **Strawberry Pieces**.

Alternately, top with chopped walnuts and sweetener to taste.

Summer Salad with Grilled Peaches, Prawns & Avocado 🍎

Serves 4

1 tbsp. **Blackened Redfish SF**

¼ tsp. **Jalapeno Powder**, optional

   Juice and zest of 1 lime

3 large ripe peaches, each sliced in 6 pieces

1 lb uncooked prawns (16-20 count),
   peeled and deveined

2 tbsp. champagne vinegar

¼ cup extra virgin olive oil
   Salt and pepper to taste

10 oz washed & dried mixed greens

1 ripe avocado, sliced root to tip

1 In a medium mixing bowl, mix the
Blackened Redfish Seasoning SF and **Jalapeno Powder** (optional) with the lime juice and zest.

2 Toss the peaches in this marinade mixture, transfer peaches to another bowl and cover. Toss the prawns in the remaining marinade, cover and refrigerate at least 15 minutes and up to 3 hours.

3 On a medium-hot grill, arrange the marinated peaches and prawns. Turn the prawns when one side is fully pink, and turn the peaches when that side begins to show a bit of char. Remove from heat as soon as each one is cooked. The prawns are done when they are pink all over and no longer translucent but not yet tightly curled up. The peaches should be cooked but not mushy.

4 Whisk together any juices left from the peaches with the vinegar, oil, salt and pepper. Toss this dressing with the lettuce.

5 Divide the lettuce, peaches, prawns & avocado evenly between 4 plates. Drizzle with remaining dressing. Serve immediately.

Milanese Risotto Cakes

1 In a small saucepan on the back of the stove, heat the chicken broth and **Saffron** to a simmer. It should maintain approximately this temperature throughout the cooking process.

2 In a large skillet, heat the olive oil over medium heat. Add the onion and cook until it becomes translucent.

3 Add the rice and stir until it begins to brown, about 3 minutes. Add the white wine and stir until most of the liquid is absorbed.

4 Add a ladle full of the broth and stir. Continue stirring frequently and adding more broth each time the rice has absorbed the previous broth. Cook in this manner for about 18 minutes or until the rice is tender.

Part 1 - Risotto
Serves 8

¼ cup extra-virgin olive oil

1 medium onion, finely diced

1 tsp. **Saffron**

2 cups Risotto Rice (Arborio, Carnaroli, or Vialone Nano)

½ cup white wine

4 cups chicken broth

2 tbsp. butter

½ cup grated Parmigiano-Reggiano cheese

5 Stir in butter and cheese. (At this point the risotto can be eaten or refrigerated for up to 2 days before making into cakes)

1 In a large bowl, combine the eggs and risotto.

2 Heat 1 tablespoon of the butter in a large skillet

3 Form the risotto mixture into 3 inch rounds (about ½ an inch thick).

4 When the butter is hot, add as many of the risotto cakes as will fit comfortably to the pan.

Part 2 - Cakes

4 tbsp. butter

5 eggs, beaten (or, if some of the risotto has been eaten, 1 egg for each cup of Risotto) Risotto from previous recipe

5 Cook on each side for about 2 to 3 minutes or until brown. Continue with the rest of the cakes, swirling another tablespoon of butter in the pan before each batch. Serve hot.

Milanese Risotto Cakes

Blackened Redfish Salmon

Serves 4

4   salmon fillets, less than ¾ inch thick

4   tbsp. butter, melted

1   tbsp. **Blackened Redfish SF**

2   tsp. **Spicy Lemon Pepper SF**

    Salt, to taste

1 Heat a large cast-iron skillet over very high heat for at least 10 minutes.

2 Combine **Blackened Redfish SF** and **Spicy Lemon Pepper SF** in a small bowl.

3 Dip each piece of fish in melted butter and sprinkle with seasoning mix generously on both sides of the fillet.

4 Place fillets in the hot skillet. Pour a small amount of butter on top of each piece of fish. Cook, uncovered, over high heat until the underside looks charred.

5 Turn the fillets over and repeat making sure the fish is cooked through. Remove to a plate and serve.

Coq au Vin

1 Dry the chicken off with a few paper towels and generously season with salt and pepper.

2 Heat the bacon in a large pot or Dutch oven over medium-high heat. When it has crisped up, remove it to a plate and add the chicken pieces to the pot. Cook for about 2 minutes on each side or until all sides are nicely browned.

3 Return the bacon to the pan and reduce the heat to medium or medium-low, depending on the heat of your stove. Cook, stirring occasionally for 5 minutes.

4 Stir in the flour and cook for 2 minutes. Add the red wine, tomato paste, garlic, **Bouquet Garni** and enough broth to mostly cover the chicken pieces.

5 Bring to a low boil, cover and reduce heat to low. Simmer gently for at least 30 minutes and up to 1½ hours (the longer it simmers, the more the flavors meld and the more tender the chicken becomes).

6 While the chicken simmers, heat the butter in a large skillet. When it is melted and begins to brown, add the pearl onions and mushrooms. Sauté until the onions begin to brown. Set aside.

7 A few minutes before serving, remove the chicken pieces from the pan. Turn the heat up to high and boil, uncovered for 5 minutes or until the sauce begins to thicken.

8 Add the mushrooms and onions and boil for another minute. Return the chicken to the pan and remove from the heat.

Serve in bowls or over polenta or egg noodles, garnished with fresh parsley.

Serves 4 - 6

3 ½ lbs of chicken pieces with bones or without, dark and light meat
Salt and pepper
4 oz of bacon in ¼ inch slices
3 tbsp. of flour
3 cups full bodied red wine
1 - 2 cups beef broth
1 tbsp. tomato paste
3 cloves garlic, finely chopped
1 tbsp. **Bouquet Garni**
3 tbsp. butter
1 lb crimini or button mushrooms, quartered
1 pound pearl onions, peeled
Fresh parsley, for garnish

Carne Asada Spiced Steak

Serves 4 by itself or 6 if used as part of tacos

3   tbsp. **Carne Asada**

3   tbsp. lime juice

½   cup olive oil

1   tbsp. sugar

1   tbsp. salt

2   pounds flank steak or skirt steak

1 In a large, re-sealable plastic bag, combine the **Carne Asada**, lime juice, olive oil, sugar and salt. Add the steak and move around until it is thoroughly coated in the marinade. Seal the bag and refrigerate for at least 3 hours and up to a day.

2 Start a hot fire in a charcoal or gas grill. When the grill is very hot, lift the meat from the marinade, brushing off any extra liquid. Grill the steak for 4 to 5 minutes on each side or until it reaches medium-rare.

3 Remove the steak from the grill and let rest for 5 minutes. Slice the meat very thinly and at an angle. Serve as the main ingredient in tacos or with a little salsa (see Zesty Salsa, 27).

Mexican Garden Salad

Serves 4 - 6

Recipe Contest Winner!
Diana from Bothell, WA

1   cup sour cream
1   16oz jar thick/chunky salsa divided in half
3   cups shredded, cooked chicken or 1 lb
    ground beef, browned & drained
1   cup water
3   tbsp. **Taco Seasoning SF**
1   head lettuce, torn into bite size pieces
3   cups broccoli florets
1   small red onion, chopped
1   avocado, cubed
1   carrot, shredded
1   large tomato, chopped
1   4oz can green chilies, drained
1   cup shredded Colby or Monterey Jack cheese
    Tortilla chips, crumbled

1 Prepare dressing by combining sour cream and 1 cup salsa. Refrigerate until ready to serve.

2 In a large skillet, combine chicken (or ground beef), remaining salsa, water and **Taco Seasoning SF**.

3 Bring to a boil and simmer 15 to 20 minutes.

4 In a large serving bowl, layer vegetables. Top with chicken mixture, chilies, cheese and dressing.

Top with crumbled chips and serve immediately.

Herbs de Provence Lamb Chops

2 tbsp. **Herbs de Provence** (or **Fine Herbs**)

1 tbsp. Dijon or whole grain mustard

2 cloves garlic

1 tsp. salt

½ tsp. pepper

¼ cup extra virgin olive oil

6 lamb chops

1 In a food processor, pulse the **Herbs de Provence**, mustard, garlic, salt and pepper until smooth.

2 Add the olive oil in a steady stream and pulse to combine.

3 Rub the paste on all sides of the lamb chops and let marinate for 1 to 6 hours in the refrigerator. Bring it back to room temperature before cooking.

4 Prepare a hot charcoal fire or heat a gas grill to high heat. Grill the lamb about 2 minutes per side for medium rare. Serve.

Chicken Piccata

Serves 4

2   lbs chicken breasts, pounded ¼ inch thick

1   tbsp. **Poultry Seasoning**

2   tbsp. olive oil

1   shallot, finely chopped

¼   cup white wine or dry sherry

2   tbsp. butter

½   lemon zest

¼   cup lemon juice

¼   cup capers, drained and rinsed

1 Rub the chicken breasts with **Poultry Seasoning**.

2 Heat the olive oil over medium-high heat in large skillet. Sauté the chicken breasts in the skillet about 4 minutes per side or until cooked through (the time will depend on the exact thickness of the chicken). When the chicken is done, remove it to a plate and cover with foil to keep hot.

3 Keeping the skillet on medium-high heat, add the shallots and sauté for 1 minute.

4 Add the white wine and stir rapidly to dissolve the browned bits on the bottom of the pan.

5 Swirl in the butter, add the lemon zest, lemon juice and capers. Cook for about 5 minutes.

Serve the chicken topped with the sauce.

Grilled Halibut 🍎

Serves 2

1   lb thick halibut fillet (substitute with your favorite fish)

1   tbsp. **Salmon Rub**

2   lemon wedges

1 Cut halibut fillet in half. Rub top generously with **Salmon Rub**.

2 Place fillets on counter top grill heated to 400°. Cook for approximately 7 to 10 minutes depending on thickness of fillet. Halibut is fully cooked when it flakes easily. Serve with lemon wedges.

Alternatively, if you don't have a counter top grill, try baking the fillets at 400° covered, for about 15 minutes or until fish flakes easily.

Classic Spaghetti with Meatballs

Serves 6
(makes 30 - 34 meatballs, depending on size)

½ lb ground pork

1 lb ground beef

1 cup bread crumbs

3 tbsp. **Spaghetti Sauce Spice**

½ cup freshly grated Parmigiano-Reggiano
   cheese

¼ tsp. black pepper

1 egg

3 tbsp. olive oil

1 onion, finely diced

1 28oz can crushed tomatoes

1 14oz can finely diced tomatoes

½ small can tomato paste

½ cup red wine

2 tbsp. **Marinara Sauce Spice**

   Salt and pepper, for seasoning

1½ lb dried spaghetti

   Freshly grated Parmigiano-Reggiano
   cheese for serving

1 Using your hands, combine the pork, beef, bread crumbs, **Spaghetti Sauce Spice**, grated cheese, pepper and egg in a large bowl until well mixed. Form into 1 inch diameter balls.

2 Heat the olive oil in a large skillet until a drop of water evaporates within a second when dropped in the oil.

3 Add the meatballs to the pan and cook until lightly browned on all sides, about 7 minutes. Remove from the pan to a plate lined with paper towels.

4 Add the onion to the pan and sauté until browned but not burnt (about 8 minutes).

5 Add the canned tomatoes, tomato paste, red wine and **Marinara Sauce Spice** and bring to a simmer. Add the meatballs to the sauce, reduce the heat to low, cover and simmer for about 20 minutes.

6 Heat a pot of boiling salted water and prepare the spaghetti according to package directions. Serve each plate of spaghetti topped with sauce and meatballs with grated Parmigiano-Reggiano sprinkled on top.

Random Tip#14

Spaghetti: When cooking spaghetti, 8 ounces of uncooked pasta
makes 4 cups cooked.

5-Spice Duck Confit with Chai Cherry Chutney & Moo Shu Pancakes

One Day Ahead:

1 Trim excess fat off the duck legs, sprinkle with a bit of the salt and place in the bottom of a glass or plastic container.

2 Place the duck legs skin side down on top of the fat, sprinkle with the remaining salt and 2 tablespoons of the **Chinese 5-Spice**.

3 Cover and refrigerate for at least 12 hours.

Day of:

1 Preheat the oven to 225°F.

2 Remove the duck from the refrigerator and pat off most of the salt with a paper towel or rinse the duck legs and pat dry.

3 Rub the rest of the **Chinese 5-Spice** on the duck legs.

4 Place the duck fat in the bottom of a heavy bottomed ovenproof pan, and then arrange the duck legs skin side down on top of the fat.

5 Pour in enough olive oil to cover the duck and place lid on pan.

6 Bake for 4 hours or until the meat is tender and pulls away from the bone. When the duck is cool enough to handle, remove it from the pot, pat off some of the oil and pull the meat off the bone into chunks.

Part 1 - Duck Confit:
Serves 6

- 4 duck leg portions, thighs attached (about 2 lbs)
- 4 tbsp. **Chinese 5-Spice**
- 2 tbsp. salt
- 4 cups olive oil or duck fat

Part 2 & 3 Continued On Next Page.

Entrees

Part 2 - Chutney:

½ cup dried sour cherries (unsweetened)
¼ cup finely chopped onion
½ cup orange juice
½ cup full-bodied red wine
1 tsp. **Chai Mix**
¼ tsp. **Cayenne 25 SHU**
¼ cup sugar

1 Combine all chutney ingredients in a small pot over medium heat.

2 Bring to a boil, reduce heat to low and simmer for 25 minutes or until thick.

Part 3 - Moo Shu Pancakes:

2 ¼ cups all-purpose flour
1 cup boiling water
3 tbsp. olive oil
¼ tsp. **13th Wonder**

Part 4 - Assembly
2 green onions, sliced in half root to tip and
   in 1 inch segments

1 Put the flour in the food processor and pour in the boiling water.

2 Pulse until the dough forms into a ball. Fifteen seconds later, add more boiling water if necessary for the dough to stick together.

3 Put the dough in a bowl, cover with a damp towel and let rest for 30 minutes.

4 Mix 2 tablespoons of the olive oil with the **13th Wonder**.

5 Turn the dough onto a lightly floured surface and cut into two pieces.

6 Put one piece to the side and cover with the damp towel.

7 Take the other piece and roll it into a rope about 12 inches long.

8 Cut the rope into 12 pieces and roll each piece into a ball. Form each ball into a two inch round.

9 Brush each one with the spiced olive oil.

10 Sandwich the rounds in pairs with the oiled sides facing each other and dust the outsides with flour.

11 Roll each sandwich into a 7 inch circle and cover with a dry cloth. Repeat with the remaining dough.

12 Heat the last tablespoon of olive oil in a medium skillet over medium-low heat. Drop one pancake into the skillet and cook until it begins to puff slightly and the underside is speckled with brown (about 1 minute).

13 Flip, and cook about 1 minute more. The pancake should be dry to the touch but not rigid.

14 Slap the hot pancake down on a cutting board. Search along the edge of the pancake and find a small opening. From there, peel the pancake apart into two pancakes. Stack the pancakes browned side down and cover with a damp cloth while cooking the rest.

To Assemble:

Make sure the duck and the chutney are either warm or at room temperature. Arrange a platter with the pancakes, duck, green onions and a bowl of chutney. Have guests wrap a few pieces of duck confit, a dollop of chutney and a few green onions in each pancake.

Braised Pork Chops with Apples, Bacon & Leeks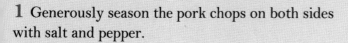

1 Generously season the pork chops on both sides with salt and pepper.

2 Heat the olive oil in a large sauté pan over medium-high heat until very hot.

3 Place the pork chops in one layer and fry on the first side until it reaches a caramel brown color, about 3 minutes. Turn the chops over and fry on the other side, about 2 minutes.

4 Remove the pork to a plate and cover with foil.

5 Add the bacon and sauté for 2 minutes or until it begins to crisp up.

6 Add the leeks with the **Italian Sausage Mix** and continue to sauté until the leeks begin to soften.

7 Add the apple cider and stir to dissolve the brown bits on the bottom of the pan. Add half of the apple, the browned pork chops and the chicken broth, enough to mostly cover the meat.

8 Bring to a simmer and reduce the heat to low. Cover and braise for 1 hour or until the pork is very tender.

9 About ten minutes before serving, add the reserved apple, cover and continue to simmer for the remaining ten minutes.

Serve each chop with plenty of sauce, rice or a good crusty bread. Top with chopped parsley if desired.

Serves 2

2   thick cut pork loin chops
    Salt and pepper
3   tbsp. olive oil
3   slices apple smoked bacon, diced
1   large leek or two medium leeks, halved root to tip and sliced into ¼ inch thick half moons
1   tsp. **Italian Sausage Mix** (add more for extra heat)
½   cup apple cider
½ – 1 cup chicken broth
1   large apple, in ½ inch dice
2   tbsp. chopped fresh parsley, optional

5-Spice Fried Rice with Tofu

Serves 4

4   tbsp. vegetable oil
1   cup mixed vegetables, chopped
1   egg, beaten
7   oz of tofu (about half a block), cut into ½
    inch pieces
4   cups leftover long grain rice (such as
    Jasmine)
2   tbsp. **Chinese 5-Spice**
2   tbsp. oyster sauce or soy sauce
½   bunch green onions, green and white
    parts, sliced ¼ inch thick

1 Heat 1 tablespoon of the oil in a large wok skillet over high heat.

2 Add the vegetables and stir-fry until they are soft and hot (times differ for each vegetable).

3 Remove the vegetables to a plate and add the egg to the wok. Cook in a pancake for one minute, and then break up and stir for another 30 seconds.

4 Remove the egg to the plate with the vegetables. Add another tablespoon of oil to the wok, then add the tofu and stir-fry until it begins to brown. Remove tofu to the vegetable plate.

5 Add the remaining 2 tablespoons of oil and then add the rice and the **Chinese 5-Spice**. Let it fry undisturbed for a minute, then break it up, and fry for another couple minutes.

6 Add the oyster sauce, vegetables, egg, tofu, green onion and stir-fry for another minute. Serve.

Tandoori-Style Chicken

Serves 4

2   tbsp. **Tandoori Masala**
1   cup plain yogurt
2   tbsp. lemon juice
1   tbsp. salt
8   chicken pieces, such as drumsticks and
    thighs (bone in)
1   green pepper, sliced into 8 pieces
2   onions, peeled and quartered

Random Tip#15

Fresh Egg Test: Fill a pan with cold water
and add some salt. Carefully place the egg in
the water. If it rises, it's old and shouldn't be
used. If it sinks to the bottom, it's fresh.

1 Combine the **Tandoori Masala** with the
yogurt, lemon juice and salt in a large re-sealable
plastic bag.

2 Add the chicken to the bag and work the bag
with your hands to coat the chicken with the
marinade.

3 Add the vegetables and toss lightly to coat
with the marinade. Refrigerate for at least 4
hours; preferably overnight.

4 Preheat the oven to 450 degrees.

5 Place the chicken and vegetables on a rack in a
roasting pan and cook for 25 minutes or until the
juices run clear when you pierce the chicken meat
near the bone. Turn once during that time.

Entrees

Vindaloo Chicken Curry with Peas

Serves 6

2 tbsp. olive oil

4 chicken breasts, cut into 1 inch pieces

1 onion, diced

1 - 2 tbsp. **Curry Powder, Vindaloo**, depending how much spice you like

1 cup tomato sauce (canned or jarred)

1 cup coconut milk

½ tsp. salt

2 cups frozen green peas

1 Heat the olive oil in large saucepan over medium-high heat. When hot, add the chicken pieces and cook on one side for 1 minute. Stir and brown for another 2 minutes. Remove to a plate and cover with foil.

2 Add the diced onion to the pan. Cook for about 3 minutes, stirring occasionally. Add the **Curry Powder, Vindaloo** and sauté for another minute.

3 Stir in the tomato sauce, coconut milk, salt, peas and reserved chicken. Simmer for 20 minutes or until the chicken is very tender.

4 Taste and season with additional **Curry Powder, Vindaloo** and salt if needed. Serve over long grain rice.

Seafood Marinade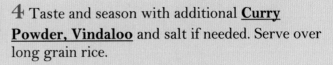

Serves 2

3 tbsp. **Seafood Seasoning**

¼ cup extra virgin olive oil

2 tbsp. white wine vinegar

2 tbsp. lemon juice

1 lb Cod fillet (or substitute for your favorite fish)

1 Combine **Seafood Seasoning**, olive oil, vinegar and lemon juice in a large container that has a lid. Cut the fillet in half if necessary.

2 Stir all the ingredients together and place fish fillet inside, making sure to coat each side of the fillet with the marinade mix.

3 Refrigerate for 1 to 2 hours before cooking and bake as desired.

Alternative: Use the Seafood Seasoning to baste your favorite fish as well. Combine 1 tablespoon Seafood Seasoning and 2 tablespoons melted butter and coat your fillet before cooking.

Kashmiri Masala Kabobs 🍎

4 – 5 skewers

3   tbsp. **Kashmiri Masala**
1   tbsp. **Sumac**
1   tsp. **Peppermint Leaves**
2   lbs lamb cut into 1 inch cubes
1   each green, red and yellow pepper, cut into 1
    inch pieces
1   red onion, cut into 1 inch pieces

1 In a sealable plastic bag, blend spices together.
Add cubed lamb and shake to coat.

2 Refrigerate for 1 to 4 hours.

3 Skewer the meat, peppers and onion, leaving 1
inch between pieces.

4 Cook on a very hot grill for several minutes on
each side.

Serve with flat bread, rice or salad.

Gnocchi with Goat Cheese Alfredo

Serves 4

1   tbsp. butter
2   tbsp. flour
1   cup whole milk
2   tbsp. **Fine Herbs**
¼   cup grated Parmigiano-Reggiano
2   oz chevre (or other cheese of your choice)
1   package gnocchi

1 Heat the butter in a small saucepan over
medium heat. When it is hot, add the flour and
whisk for 45 seconds.

2 Add the milk and **Fine Herbs** all at once and
whisk together for 4 minutes. Strain out the
herbs.

3 Bring back to a boil and add the cheeses. Whisk
rapidly until the cheese is melted and combined.
Remove from heat.

4 Prepare the gnocchi according to package
directions. Toss with the cheese sauce.

Tunisian Lamb & Apricot Stew with Couscous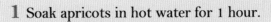

1 Soak apricots in hot water for 1 hour.

2 Heat the olive oil in a large sauté pan over medium-high heat until very hot.

3 Add onions and celery to the pan and stir for about 5 minutes or until starting to brown.

4 Add **Berbere**, **Harissa**, **Cinnamon Stick**, currants, soaked apricots and lamb. Stir to heat adding broth and pomegranate molasses.

5 Lower heat to very low and simmer for three hours or until the lamb is very soft. Stir in toasted almonds. Remove **Cinnamon Stick**.

6 Right before serving, prepare Couscous.

Part 1 - Stew:
Serves 6:

1	cup dried apricots
1	tbsp. olive oil
1 ½	lbs boneless lamb shoulder meat in ½ inch cubes
2	onions, diced
2	celery stalks, thinly sliced
1	tbsp. **Berbere (Ethiopian All-Purpose)**
1	tbsp. **Harissa Seasoning** (add more to taste)
1	**6" Cinnamon Stick**
3	tbsp. currants
1	cup chicken broth
2	tbsp. pomegranate molasses (substitute concentrated cranberry juice if pomegranate molasses is unavailable)
1	cup toasted, slivered almonds

Part 2 - Couscous:

2	cups water
2	cups whole wheat couscous

1 Boil the water. When it boils, stir in the couscous, remove from heat and cover for 10 minutes. Fluff with a fork. Serve with stew.

Random Tip#16

Tenderizing: Use 2 cups of your favorite hot tea as a cooking liquid to tenderize pot roasts or stewing meats.

Pictured with Harissa Grilled Vegetables, 116

Entrees

Smokey BBQ Pork Spareribs

For Ribs:

1   rack of pork spareribs
2   tbsp. **Smokey Meat Rub**
2   cups hickory wood chips, soaked for 1 hour in cold water (optional)

1 With disposable gloves, rub **Smokey Meat Rub** on ribs at least 3 hours before barbequing. Wrap in plastic wrap and refrigerate until time to cook.

2 Heat the oven to 225°F. Bake ribs in a roasting pan for 2 to 3 hours.

3 Begin BBQ Sauce an hour before serving.

Hickory Wood Chip Method:

1 If using, place the wood chips in an aluminum foil bowl or box on top gas grill burners. Be sure to prepare BBQ Sauce beforehand so it's available when needed.

2 Heat the grill with all flames on high. When hot, turn off flames on one half of the grill and turn the other half to medium heat.

3 Place the ribs on the side without flames and close the lid. Flip the ribs after 30 minutes.

4 After 20 more minutes, baste the ribs with barbeque sauce. After ten minutes, remove the ribs from heat, wrap in aluminum foil, put in a paper bag, and let rest for 30 minutes to an hour.

For Barbeque Sauce:

2   tbsp. vegetable oil
1   onion, finely diced
1   can diced tomatoes, drained
2   tbsp. cider vinegar
1   tbsp. **Worcestershire Powder**
3   tbsp. **Barbeque Spice SF**

1 Heat the oil in a small saucepan over medium heat.

2 Add the onion. Cook for 10 minutes or until caramelized.

3 Add the tomatoes, cider vinegar, **Worcestershire Powder** and **Barbeque Spice SF**. Simmer for 1 hour. Puree in a blender until smooth.

Serve with ribs.

Random Tip#17
Marinating: Marinate red meats in wine to tenderize.

Pictured with Red Cabbage & Green Papaya Slaw, 110, 111

Entrees

Watercress Salad with Spicy Tuna

1 In a small bowl, whisk together the lemon juice, lemon zest, 3 tablespoons of olive oil, ½ teaspoon of salt and 1 teaspoon of **Japanese 7-Spice** for dressing.

2 On a plate, mix together 3 tablespoons of **Japanese 7-Spice** and 1 ½ teaspoon salt.

3 Coat the tuna steaks in the remaining 2 tablespoons of olive oil and then transfer to the plate. Lightly coat the tuna on all sides with the spice; the thicker the coat the spicier the tuna.

4 Heat a large skillet over high heat. When hot, add the tuna to the pan and sear for 1 or 2 minutes per side, depending on the thickness of the steak and how rare you like your tuna. Remove from the pan, cool for a couple minutes, and then slice thinly.

Serves 4

2 tbsp. lemon juice
   Zest of 1 lemon
5 tbsp. olive oil
½ tsp. plus 1 ½ tsp. salt
1 tsp. plus 3 tbsp. **Japanese 7-Spice** (less to taste)
½ lb tuna steaks
1 large bunch watercress, washed and tough stems removed
1 green onion, thinly sliced (green and white parts)

5 Toss the watercress with the dressing. Divide the salad between 4 plates, and top each salad with a few slices of seared tuna. Sprinkle with the green onions and serve.

Green Herb Pan-Fried Sea Bass

Serves 2

1   lb sea bass fillets (or substitute for your favorite fish)
¼   cup flour
1   tbsp. **Green Herb Seafood Seasoning SF**
¼   cup vegetable oil

1 In a small mixing bowl combine the flour and **Green Herb Seafood Seasoning SF** and blend together.

2 Coat the fish fillets with the seasoned flour.

3 In a large frying pan fry the fish in ¼ inch of hot oil, turning until browned on both sides, approximately 6 to 8 minutes

Serve hot with lemon wedges.

Harissa Dipped Steak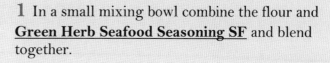

1 In a sauce pan, combine **Harissa Seasoning**, water and olive oil. Bring to a low simmer, stirring constantly. If sauce becomes too thick, add water to dilute.

Serves 4

½   cup **Harissa Seasoning**
½   cup water
2   tbsp. olive oil
2   lbs steak of choice

2 Pour sauce into air-tight container and refrigerate until ready to use.

3 Salt and pepper steak as desired and grill over hot coals, preferably slightly rare on the inside and slightly charred on the outside.

4 Slice the steak into thin strips.

5 Pour the Harissa Sauce (hot or cold) into a dish and serve with the steak as a dip.

Alternately, marinate the steaks overnight in the Harissa Sauce and grill as desired.

Random Tip#18
Tuna: Add ½ tsp. per can of tuna of any **Curry Powder** made by MarketSpice for a lively tasting tuna sandwich.

Seared Duck Breast with Rhubarb Sauce

Serves 4

4   duck breasts, preferably Muscovy
1   tbsp. plus ½ tsp. salt
¼   cup **Herbs de Provence**
2   tbsp. olive oil
½   lb rhubarb, sliced ¼ inch thick
½   cup sugar

1 Lay the duck breasts skin side down on a cutting board. Trim off any additional fat showing around the edges. Flip them over. Being careful not to pierce the meaty part of the duck, use a sharp paring knife to score the skin in a crosshatch pattern. The slices should be about a half inch apart and should go about ⅛ inch deep.

2 On a plate, combine 1 tablespoon salt and the **Herbs de Provence**. Transfer the duck breasts to the plate, turning to completely coat in the herb mixture. Cover with plastic wrap and allow the flavors to meld for 15 minutes at room temperature.

3 Meanwhile, place the rhubarb, sugar and remaining ½ teaspoon salt in a small saucepan over medium-low heat. Cook, stirring frequently until the rhubarb is soft and has released its juices.

4 Heat the olive oil in a skillet large enough for all the duck to fit in one layer over medium-low heat. When the oil is hot, add the duck breasts to the skillet skin side down.

5 Cook for 10 to 12 minutes or until most of the fat has rendered out of the skin. Remove most of the fat from the pan, reserving 1 tablespoon. Flip the duck breasts and cook for about 2 to 3 minutes on the other side or until medium rare.

6 Stir the reserved duck fat and any herbs left on the bottom of the duck cooking skillet into the rhubarb sauce.

Serve each duck breast with a generous spoonful of sauce.

Entrees

Mahi Mahi Fish Tacos
with Mango Salsa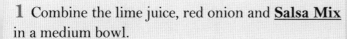

1 Combine the lime juice, red onion and **Salsa Mix** in a medium bowl.

2 Stir in the mango, Anaheim pepper, tomato and cilantro.

3 Let the lime juice mellow the onion for about 15 minutes.

4 Let the flavors meld at room temperature for up to an hour or cover and refrigerate for up to 2 days.

Part 1 - Mango Salsa:

¼ cup lime juice
½ red onion, finely diced
½ tsp. **Salsa Mix**
2 ripe mangos, peeled, seeded and diced
½ Anaheim pepper, seeded and diced
1 small tomato, diced
¼ cup cilantro, chopped

Part 2 - Brining & Grilling Fish:

¼ cup sugar
2 tbsp. salt
2 cups water
2 filets Mahi Mahi or other firm fleshed
   white fish
2 tbsp. **Taco Seasoning SF**
2 tbsp. lime juice

1 In a medium bowl, dissolve the sugar and salt in the water. Add the filets to the brine and refrigerate for 30 minutes or up to an hour.

2 Remove the fish filets and rub them with the **Taco Seasoning SF** and lime juice.

3 Prepare a grill on medium heat. Grill the fish for about 5 minutes per side or until the outside is slightly charred and the fish is no longer transparent in the middle. Remove to a plate and break the fish into chunks.

1 Heat the tortillas in the microwave for 30 seconds.

2 Smear about 1 teaspoon of avocado along the center line of each tortilla. Add some lettuce, a few pieces of fish and top with Mango Salsa. Serve warm.

Part 3 - Preparing Tacos:
Makes 12 tacos

12 corn tortillas
½ avocado, stirred with a fork to make a
   puree/paste
2 cups shredded lettuce

Perfect Turkey Brine with Gravy

Part 1 - Turkey:

1 gallon cold water

½ cup salt

½ cup **Brown Sugar**

1 - 2 tbsp. **Turkey Brine Mix**

1 non-reactive container, large enough to
   submerge turkey

1 12-14 lb unseasoned Turkey, leg restraints
   and giblets removed

1 Mix **Brown Sugar** & **Turkey Brine Mix** with
water in the non-reactive container until dissolved.
Place the turkey breast-side down into the brine.
Place a heavy plate or bowl onto the turkey to keep
it submerged. Add more cold water if necessary to
cover.

2 Refrigerate for 8 hours. While brining, turkey
must be kept below 40°. Add ice if necessary.

3 About an hour before cooking, remove the
turkey from the brine. Rinse it under cold water and
pat dry with paper towels.

4 Tuck the wings under the body and apply a light coat of olive oil to the entire bird. Sprinkle more
Turkey Brine on the bird inside and out.

5 Roast at 325° until it reaches an internal temperature of 160° to 165° in the breast and 170° to 175°
in the thigh (approximately 2 ½ to 3 hours). When the turkey is done, let rest for 30 minutes before
carving. Save drippings for gravy.

1 Place the turkey roasting pan on the stovetop over
medium-high heat with the drippings still in the pan.

2 Whisk in the flour and continue whisking until the
flour just begins to brown.

3 Whisk in the **Game Hen Blend** until combined,
then add the white wine and whisk until smooth.

4 Add the broth in a steady stream, whisking to keep
the gravy smooth. Bring the gravy to a simmer and
let cook for another 5 minutes or until it thickens.

5 Stir in any juices/drippings that have gathered as
you sliced the turkey. Pour into a gravy boat and serve.

Part 2 - Gravy:
Makes 6 cups

¼ cup flour

2 tsp. **Game Hen Blend**

½ cup white wine (substitute water if you
   don't want to open a bottle of wine)

6 cups low sodium turkey or chicken broth
   Drippings from roasting a turkey

Japanese 7-Spice Soba Noodles

Serves 6

14 oz package soba noodles
1   tbsp. sesame oil
1   can chickpeas, drained and rinsed
1   tbsp. **Japanese 7-Spice**
3   green onions, thinly sliced

1 Heat a pot of salted water to boiling. Add the soba noodles and boil gently for about 4 minutes. Drain and set aside.

2 Heat the sesame oil in a large skillet over medium-high heat. When hot, add the chickpeas and sauté for 4 minutes or until they are fully hot and begin to darken.

3 Add half the **Japanese 7-Spice** and stir. Add the soba noodles, toss to combine and add the rest of the **Japanese 7-Spice**.

4 Toss again, transfer to plates and top with a generous sprinkling of sliced green onions before serving.

Entrees

Andouille, Chicken & Prawn Gumbo

1 Heat 1 tablespoon of the vegetable oil in a large saucepan over medium–high heat.

2 Add the chicken and sausages. Brown for 1 minute without stirring; then stir occasionally for 5 minutes or until mostly cooked. Remove the meat and place in a covered bowl while cooking the roux.

3 Add ½ cup vegetable oil to the pan. When the oil is hot enough that a drop of water sizzles off within a second or two, add the flour all at once and whisk thoroughly.

4 Reduce the heat to medium and continue whisking regularly for the next 15 to 25 minutes or until the roux reaches a deep brown color.

5 Add the onion, celery and bell pepper to the roux. Reduce heat to low and stir for 3 minutes.

6 Add the two broths, chicken, sausage and **Cajun Seasoning**. Gently simmer the gumbo uncovered for 1 hour. Then cover for at least 1 hour and up to 6 hours.

7 While the gumbo is cooking, heat a pot of salted water to boiling. Add the okra and boil for 5 minutes. Drain in a colander.

Serves 6

½ cup plus 1 tbsp. vegetable oil

¾ lb boneless skinless chicken (breast, thigh, or combination) cut into large bite-size pieces

2 Andouille sausages, sliced half inch thick

¾ cup all-purpose flour

1 onion, finely chopped

2 celery stalks, finely chopped

½ green bell pepper, finely chopped

4 cups chicken broth

1 cup clam broth (or substitute more chicken broth)

1 heaping tbsp. **Cajun Seasoning**

½ lb okra, sliced a half inch thick and rinsed

½ tbsp. **Gumbo Filé**

1 lb prawns or large shrimp, peeled and deveined

Add water or chicken broth, if necessary to thin

8 About 10 minutes before serving time, add the boiled okra and uncooked prawns to the gumbo. Continue to simmer.

9 Right before serving, sprinkle on the **Gumbo Filé** and stir to combine. If you think the gumbo is too thick, add extra chicken broth or water to bring it to the desired consistency. Serve over long-grain rice.

Entrees

Mediterranean Capellini with Prawns, Feta & Cherry Tomatoes

Serves 5

¾ lb angel hair pasta

2 tbsp. extra virgin olive oil

1 pint cherry tomatoes sliced in half or 1 can diced tomatoes

1 tbsp. **Greek Seasoning**

8 oz fresh feta cheese, crumbled

1 lb. raw large shrimp, peeled and deveined

2 tbsp. chopped fresh parsley, optional

1 Heat a pot of salted water over high heat. Cook the angel hair pasta according to package directions. Begin the sauce while the pasta is cooking.

2 Heat the olive oil in a large skillet over medium heat. Add the tomatoes and **Greek Seasoning**. Sauté until the tomatoes release their juices and begin to turn to a sauce. Add the feta.

3 Bring back to a simmer and cook until the sauce becomes creamy. Add the shrimp until it turns pink and begins to curl.

4 Toss the sauce with the angel hair, garnish with the parsley and serve.

Seasoned Taco Meat

1 lb ground beef

2 tsp. **Taco Seasoning SF**

2 tsp. flour

½ tsp. salt

½ cup water

1 In a large skillet over medium heat, brown the beef and drain out the fat.

2 In a separate bowl blend together the **Taco Seasoning SF**, flour and salt.

3 Reduce heat to low and add the seasoning mixture into the skillet stirring continuously for about half a minute.

4 Add the water and cook for another 10 minutes or until the mixture is thickened.

Use for tacos, nachos, enchiladas, taco burgers, salads and casseroles.

Za'atar Roast Chicken with Root Vegetables

1 Preheat the oven to 450°F.

2 In a small bowl, combine the **Za'atar Blend**, salt, mustard, 2 tablespoons of the olive oil and garlic to create a thick paste.

3 Thoroughly wash your chicken inside and out with cold water and pat dry with paper towels.

4 Tuck the wingtips back behind their first joints. Using your fingers and starting at the bottom of the breast, carefully loosen the skin from the meat. Take about a tablespoon of the Za'atar paste and work it under the skin as far in as possible. Take another couple tablespoons and cover the entire surface of the bird in the paste. Use any leftover herb paste to get more underneath the skin. Tie the legs together with kitchen twine.

Serves 4

- ¼ cup **Za'atar Blend**
- 1 tbsp. salt
- 2 tbsp. Dijon mustard
- 4 tbsp. olive oil
- 5 cloves garlic, finely chopped
- 1 whole chicken, 3½ lbs to 4 lbs, giblets removed
- 4 cups root vegetables, peeled and cut into ½ inch slices (such as yellow beets, parsnips, potatoes, carrots, onions)
- 1 tbsp. **Salish Alderwood Smoked Salt**, lightly ground

5 In the bottom of a large roasting pan with a rack, spread the vegetables. Drizzle with the remaining 2 tablespoons olive oil and season with the **Salish Alderwood Smoked Salt**.

6 Place the rack in the pan and put the chicken on the rack, breast side up. Roast until the juices run clear when the thickest part of the thigh is pierced with a knife (it will be about 165° to 170°F), about one hour.

7 Remove from the oven and let rest for ten minutes. To serve, transfer the chicken to a serving platter, toss the vegetables in the pan juices and place them around the chicken.

Random Tip#19
Cooking Vegetables: Never overcook as this will
cause them to lose flavor, texture and vitamins.

Entrees

Crabcakes with Cajun Remoulade & Fried Green Tomatoes

1 In a food processor, blend the egg yolks, lemon juice, celery, green onion, parsley and **Cajun Seasoning** for about 10 seconds.

2 With the food processor running, add ¾ cup olive oil in a steady stream and process until the sauce thickens to a loose mayonnaise, about 1 minute. Cover and refrigerate.

Part 1 - Rémoulade:

2 egg yolks (reserve one egg white for the crabcakes)
2 tbsp. lemon juice
¼ cup celery
1 green onion, sliced
2 tbsp. parsley
2 tsp. **Cajun Seasoning**
¾ cup olive oil

1 In a medium mixing bowl, soak the sliced green tomatoes in the buttermilk. In another medium bowl, mix the cornmeal, flour, salt and **Fine Black Pepper**.

2 Heat two tablespoons of olive oil in a frying pan. Take a tomato slice from the buttermilk, coat it on both sides with the cornmeal mixture and place in the hot frying pan.

3 Repeat with the remaining slices, adding additional oil as needed. Fry the tomatoes on both sides until they brown nicely but do not burn. Reserve, covered with foil, until serving time.

Part 2 - Fried Green Tomatoes:

4 small or 2 large green tomatoes, sliced
2 cups buttermilk
½ cup finely ground cornmeal
½ cup all-purpose flour
½ tsp. salt
¼ tsp. **Fine Black Pepper**
2 tbsp. olive oil

Part 3 - Crabcakes:

¼ cup breadcrumbs, plus ½ cup for coating
1 egg white
½ lb crabmeat
1 tbsp. olive oil

1 In a small mixing bowl, combine the bread crumbs, egg white and ¼ cup of the rémoulade. Let soak for 10 minutes.

2 Place the crabmeat in a strainer and gently squeeze out the excess liquid. Combine the crabmeat and the bread crumb mixture.

3 Form into six small crabcakes and place on a plate of breadcrumbs. Turn once to coat both sides.

4 Heat 1 tablespoon of olive oil in a medium skillet. Add the crabcakes and fry until browned on one side, flip and brown the second side. The crabcakes are done when it is lightly browned and heated through.

Serves 6 as an appetizer and 4 as a light main course. Serve with a dollop of rémoulade and a few slices of fried green tomatoes.

Random Tip#20
"After Cooking" Seasonings: **Black Pepper**, **Garlic Powder** or **Garlic Granules**, **Salt,** and **Cayenne Pepper (25, 50 & 100 SHU)** are excellent "after cooking" seasonings. Allow individuals to season dishes with these spices at the table.

BREADS & SIDES

Kashmiri Lentils

Serves 4

1   cup lentils (preferably de Puy or other
    French-style lentils)
2 ½ cups chicken broth or water
1   tsp. salt (omit if using chicken broth)
1   tbsp. **Kashmiri Masala**

1 Combine all ingredients in a small saucepan over high heat. Bring to a boil, cover and reduce heat to low.

2 Simmer for 30 minutes or until fully cooked. Serve.

Random Tip#21
Spice/Herb Substitutions: If you're feeling adventurous, try replacing herbs & spices called for in recipes with something different: **Marjoram** instead of **Oregano**, **Savory** instead of **Thyme**, **Cilantro** instead of **Parsley**, **Anise Seed** instead of **Fennel Seed**, etc.

Shaved Fennel, Apple & Pomegranate Salad 🍎

Serves 4

2 tbsp. white wine vinegar

¼ cup extra virgin olive oil

1 tbsp. **Yogurt Dill Dressing Mix**

½ tsp. salt

1 crisp apple, sliced into matchsticks

1 fennel bulb, sliced very thinly
   Seeds from 1 pomegranate

½ cup hazelnuts, toasted, peeled and
   chopped (optional)

1 In a large bowl, whisk together the vinegar, oil, **Yogurt Dill Dressing Mix** and salt.

2 Add the sliced apple, fennel and pomegranate seeds. Toss to combine.

Top with the hazelnuts and serve.

Red Cabbage & Green Papaya Slaw

Serves 10

2 tbsp. **Coleslaw Spice**
¼ cup vegetable oil
¼ cup lime juice
½ tsp. salt
2 tbsp. honey
  Half a small red cabbage, thinly sliced, makes about 4 cups
  Half a small green papaya, grated with the grated attachment to a food processor, makes about 2 cups
½ cup cilantro

1 In a large bowl, combine the **Coleslaw Spice**, vegetable oil, lime juice, salt and honey.

2 Add the cabbage, green papaya and cilantro. Toss well.

3 Let stand for 30 minutes at room temperature or up to 2 days in the refrigerator before serving.

Spicy Lemon Pepper Green Beans

1 lb fresh green beans, cut into 2 inch lengths
2 tbsp. butter
2 tbsp. minced fresh parsley
2 tsp. **Spicy Lemon Pepper SF**
  Salt, to taste

1 Cook beans uncovered in rapidly boiling, salted water until slightly tender, about 6 to 8 minutes.

2 Drain and immediately immerse in a bowl of cold water with a few ice cubes until cold to the touch. Drain and refrigerate until ready to serve.

3 Before serving, combine butter, parsley and **Spicy Lemon Pepper SF** in a skillet.

4 Place over medium-high heat and add the green beans.

5 Toss until heated through. Season with salt to taste.

Red Cabbage & Green Papaya Slaw pictured with Smokey BBQ Pork Spareribs, 88, 89

Breads & Sides

Fruit Butter & Nut Muffins

Makes 12 muffins

2 cups flour

2 tsp. baking powder

1 cup vanilla yogurt

½ cup milk

4 tbsp. melted butter

1 egg

½ cup finely chopped pecans

2 tbsp. **MarketSpice Cinnamon-Orange Creamed Honey**

1 jar **MarketSpice Apple-Fruit Butter**

1 Preheat oven to 400°F. Line a muffin tin with paper cups.

2 Stir the flour and baking powder together in large mixing bowl.

3 Stir in the yogurt, milk, melted butter, egg, pecans and **MarketSpice Cinnamon-Orange Creamed Honey**.

4 Fill each muffin paper half full. Add a dollop of **MarketSpice Apple-Fruit Butter** to each muffin and cover with the remaining batter.

5 Bake for 20 minutes or until golden.

Serve warm.

Easy & Healthy Popcorn 🍎

½ cup popcorn kernels

1 tsp. olive oil

½ tsp. salt (if desired)

1 tbsp. **Healthy Heart Seasoning SF** (or your favorite seasoning)

1 Mix everything together in a medium bowl.

2 Pour into a kraft paper bag (6 x 4 x 12 works well).

3 Fold top over twice and shake well to coat all kernels.

4 Microwave until popping stops. Approximately 2½ to 3 minutes depending on your microwave.

5 Pour into bowl and serve.

Alternative: Simply microwave your favorite brand of pre-bagged popcorn and add olive oil and seasoning. To remain healthy, use unbuttered and unsalted bag.

Random Tip#22
Garlic Odor: Rub your hands with salt to remove garlic odor.

Provençale Savory Bread Pudding

Serves 8 - 10

1   tbsp. butter, softened
5   eggs
2 ½ cups lowfat or whole milk
2   tbsp. balsamic vinegar
¼   tsp. salt
¼   tsp. **Fine Black Pepper**
2   tbsp. olive oil
2   tbsp. **Fine Herbs**
1   loaf French or sourdough bread (about 17 ounces), cut into 1 inch cubes
½   cup Kalamata olives, sliced
½   cup sundried tomatoes, thinly sliced
½   red onion, thinly sliced root to tip
½   cup goat cheese, crumbled

1 Preheat the oven to 375°F.

2 Grease a 9" by 13" glass or metal ovenproof dish with the softened butter.

3 In a large mixing bowl, beat together the eggs, milk, vinegar, salt, pepper, olive oil and **Fine Herbs**.

4 Add the bread cubes, olives, sundried tomatoes, red onions and goat cheese.

5 Stir to combine and let rest for a few minutes while the bread soaks up the egg mixture.

6 Transfer the egg and bread mixture to the prepared baking dish.

7 Bake for 30 minutes or until golden brown.

Cool slightly before serving. Pairs well with pork or chicken.

Breads & Sides

Harissa Grilled Vegetables

Serves 6

1 tbsp. olive oil
1 tbsp. **Harissa Seasoning**
1 tsp. water
½ eggplant, sliced
2 small zucchinis, sliced lengthwise
½ red onion, in wedges
½ yellow bell pepper, sliced thin
½ red bell pepper, sliced thin
2 small tomatoes, halved

1 Stir together the olive oil, **Harissa Seasoning** and water.

2 Toss the vegetables in this paste.

3 Cook in a grill basket on a hot grill for 15 minutes, or until vegetables are fully cooked.

Iranian Wild Rice Pilaf

Serves 6

2 cups wild rice
4 cups chicken broth or water
1 ¼ cups frozen baby lima beans
2 tbsp. **Iranian Rice Blend**
   Salt and pepper to taste

1 Heat the broth in a medium saucepan over high heat.

2 Add the wild rice, lima beans and **Iranian Rice Blend** to the boiling water.

3 When the mixture returns to a boil, reduce the heat to medium-low, cover and simmer for 35 minutes.

Adjust seasoning with salt and pepper and serve.

Random Tip#23
Corn on the Cob: A dampened paper towel or
terry cloth brushed downward on a cob of corn
will remove every strand of corn silk.

Harissa Grilled Vegetables pictured with Tunisian Lamb & Apricot Stew, 86

Breads & Sides

Green Spinach Salad

Part 1 - Dressing:

1 tbsp. balsamic vinegar

1 tbsp. lemon juice

¼ tsp. **Greek Seasoning**

¼ cup extra virgin olive oil

2 tsp. Dijon mustard

Salt and pepper to taste

1 Whisk all the dressing ingredients together and let rest for at least 5 minutes while you assemble the salad.

Part 2 - Salad:
Serves 4

1 bag washed baby spinach

4 oz fresh feta cheese, crumbled

1 stalk celery, thinly sliced

1 English cucumber, thinly sliced

½ cup Kalamata olives

½ cup artichoke hearts

1 tomato, sliced

1 small jar roasted red peppers, drained and sliced

½ red onion, sliced

1 Arrange the salad makings in a large bowl. Toss with the dressing and serve immediately.

Breads & Sides

Homemade Tortilla Chips

1 Stack the tortillas and cut them in half. Cut them in ¼ inch slices the opposite direction, to make many tortilla strips.

4 corn tortillas, preferably a bit stale
2 cups peanut or corn oil
1 tbsp. **Seasoned Salt**, more to taste

2 Heat about 2 inches of oil in a small or medium saucepan over medium-high heat. Heat the oil until it is hot enough that when you put a dry wooden spoon in the oil, little bubbles immediately rise from the spoon.

3 Carefully add half the tortilla strips to the hot oil. Cook, turning occasionally until they turn a light golden brown.

4 Using a slotted spoon, remove the tortilla chips to a paper towel-lined plate. Repeat with the remaining tortilla bits. Sprinkle with **Seasoned Salt**.

Homemade Tortilla Chips pictured with Mexicali Tortilla Soup, 46

Panch Phoron Vegetables

2 tbsp. olive oil
3 tsp. **Panch Phoron Mix**
1 medium onion, chopped
1 large yam, cubed
2 large red potatoes
2 small russet potatoes

1 Heat the olive oil in a large skillet.

2 Add **Panch Phoron Mix** to pan and stir for two minutes to blend.

3 Add vegetables and sauté until potatoes reach desired tenderness.

9-Spice Rice

Serves 2 to 4

2 tbsp. olive oil
½ onion, chopped
½ red bell pepper, chopped
1 cup **Long Grain Rice** (included in 9-Spice For Rice package)
½ cup white wine
1 **9-Spice Rice Seasoning** (included in 9-Spice For Rice package)
2 cups water

1 Heat the olive oil in a medium saucepan over medium-high heat.

2 Add the onion and red bell pepper and sauté until onion becomes translucent.

3 Add **Long Grain Rice** and stir for 2 to 3 minutes or until rice begins to brown.

4 Add white wine and stir to scrape up any bits stuck to the bottom of the pan.

5 Add water and **9-Spice Rice Seasoning**. When the mixture returns to a boil, reduce the heat to low and cover.

6 Simmer about 20 minutes or until the rice is cooked.

Random Tip#24
Rice: 1 cup uncooked long grain makes
3 cups cooked.

Apple Chutney

Makes 2 cups

4   large tart apples, cored and cut into ½ inch
     dice (peel them if you like)
½   onion, finely diced
¼   cup white wine vinegar
2   tbsp. balsamic vinegar
2   tbsp. sugar
¼   cup dried cherries or raisins
1   tsp. **Chutney Mix**

1 Combine all ingredients in a medium saucepan over high heat.

2 When it begins to boil, reduce heat to medium-low and simmer for 20 minutes.

Serve as a side with meat dishes, especially pork chops.

Greek Garlic Bread ⭐

Makes 1 loaf of garlic bread

1   stick salted butter, softened
2   tbsp. **Greek Seasoning**
1   loaf crusty olive bread

1 Heat the oven to 400°F. Combine softened butter and **Greek Seasoning** in a small bowl and whip with a fork.

2 Slice the olive bread in half horizontally and spread the butter mixture on both cut sides of the bread. Close the loaf and wrap it in aluminum foil.

3 Bake for 15 minutes. Serve warm.

Random Tip#25

Ground Turkey: When using ground turkey as a healthier alternative to beef, add 1 tablespoon **Beef Soup Base** for a beefy taste. Note: Always purchase "lean" ground turkey, or you will have as much or more fat content than ground beef.

Smokey Corn Muffins
with Chipotle Honey Butter

1 Preheat oven to 350°F. Rinse ears and place corn husk on the middle rack of oven.

2 Bake for 30 minutes.

3 Remove corn husks from cob and cut kernels off into a bowl. Save ½ cup for muffins.

Part 1 - Corn:

1   corn husk

Part 2 - Corn Muffins:
Serves 8

2   eggs
1   cup buttermilk
1   cup cornmeal
1   cup flour
2   tsp. baking powder
½   tsp. salt
1   tsp. **Chipotle Chili Pepper**
5   tbsp. unsalted butter, melted
1   tbsp. softened butter for the muffin tins

1 Turn up oven to 400°F. Grease muffin tin with 1 tablespoon butter.

2 Beat eggs into the buttermilk in a large mixing bowl.

3 In a small mixing bowl, sift together the flour, baking powder and salt. Stir in the cornmeal and **Chipotle Chili Pepper**.

4 Whisk the cornmeal mixture into the buttermilk mixture. Add the melted butter and whisk to combine. Stir in the corn.

5 Distribute the batter evenly among the 12 muffins. Bake for about 12 minutes or until the muffins begin to brown. Serve warm with Honey Butter.

1 With a fork, stir the honey and **Chipotle Chili Pepper** into the butter. Set aside until serving time.

Part 3 - Honey Butter:

3   tbsp. butter, softened
2   tbsp. honey
¼ - ½ tsp. **Chipotle Chili Pepper**, to taste

DESSERTS

Cinnamon-Orange Flan

1 Preheat the oven to 350°F.

2 Set 6 ramekins (about ½ cups size) in a 9 by 13 inch baking dish.

3 In a small saucepan, heat ½ cup of sugar with the water over medium-high heat, stirring until the sugar dissolves. Without stirring, bring the sugar to a boil. When it begins to color, swirl the pan some but still do not stir. When the syrup reaches a golden caramel color, remove from heat and evenly distribute the syrup between the ramekins. Lift each ramekin and swirl the caramel a bit to coat the bottom.

Makes 6 individual servings

½ cup plus 3 tbsp. sugar
¼ cup water
1 cup heavy cream
1 cup whole milk
3 tbsp. **MarketSpice Cinnamon-Orange Black Tea** leaves
1 large egg
3 large egg yolks
Boiling water
6 Ramekins

4 In a medium saucepan over medium-heat, bring the heavy cream, milk and remaining 3 tablespoons sugar just to a boil. Stir in the **MarketSpice Cinnamon Orange Black Tea** leaves, remove from heat, cover and steep for 10 minutes. Strain the milk mixture to remove the tea leaves.

5 In a medium mixing bowl, beat together the egg and egg yolks.

6 Slowly add ¼ cup of the milk and tea mixture, whisking to combine. Add the remaining milk mixture and whisk together.

7 Distribute this mixture evenly between the ramekins.

8 Add enough boiling water to the baking pan to reach halfway up the ramekins, being careful not to splash any into the custards.

9 Bake the custards for about 50 minutes or until they are set all the way through.

10 Remove the ramekins from the water bath and allow to cool.

11 Refrigerate for at least an hour and up to a day before serving.

To serve, take one flan, run a sharp knife around the edge to loosen, and turn it upside down on a small plate. Or, for simplicity, serve them out of the ramekins.

Coconut Oolong Pudding

1 Heat the milk in a medium saucepan over medium heat until it begins to boil, stirring frequently to keep the milk from burning on the bottom of the pan.

2 Remove from heat, add the **Jade Spring Oolong Tea** leaves and cover. Steep for 7 minutes and strain out the tea leaves, pressing as much liquid out of the leaves as possible.

3 Meanwhile, stir together the cornstarch and sugar in a small mixing bowl. Whisk vigorously while slowly pouring in 1 cup of the coconut milk. The mixture should be smooth.

4 Add the remaining coconut milk to the milk in the saucepan and return to medium heat. When it begins to boil, whisk while slowly pouring in the cornstarch, sugar and coconut milk mixture. Add the shredded coconut.

5 Continue stirring until the pudding begins to thicken, about 4 minutes.

6 Remove from heat and chill for at least an hour before serving.

Garnish with tangerine and blood orange slices.

Serves 6 - 8

2	cups whole or 2% milk
2	tbsp. **Jade Spring Oolong Tea** leaves
¼	cup cornstarch
½	cup sugar
2	cups coconut milk
½	cup shredded coconut

Desserts

Chewy Chocolate Ginger Cookies 🎀

Recipe Contest Winner!
Maryon from Lakeland, FL

Makes 36 cookies

1   stick butter, unsalted

4   oz unsweetened baking chocolate, chopped

1 ½ cups granulated sugar

1 ½ cups all-purpose flour

½   cup **Pernigotti Cocoa Powder**

1   tsp. baking powder

1   tsp. baking soda

½   tsp. salt

3   eggs, beaten

¾   cup **Candied Ginger**, finely chopped

½   cup mini semisweet chocolate chips

1   cup powdered sugar

1 Preheat oven to 350°F.

2 In a medium saucepan, melt butter and unsweetened chopped chocolate. Cool for 10 minutes.

3 In a large bowl, sift together granulated sugar, flour, **Pernigotti Cocoa Powder**, baking powder, baking soda and salt.

4 Whisk the beaten eggs into the cooled butter/chocolate mixture. Be sure to let the butter/chocolate mixture cool or you will cook the eggs.

5 Stir egg mixture with the dry ingredients. Stir in chopped **Candied Ginger** and chocolate chips.

6 Shape into 1" balls. Roll in powdered sugar. Place 2" apart on two non-stick baking sheets or baking sheets coated with non-stick cooking spray.

7 Bake, rotating the pans between shelves after 10 minutes for 14 to 17 minutes total.

8 Remove when the cookies are puffy and cracked on the top. Let cool on pan for 1 minute, then remove to baking rack to continue cooling.

Store in an air-tight container.

Random Tip#26 💡
Vanilla Powder: Use **Vanilla Powder** in place of liquid extract vanilla when baking, making icings or whipping cream. Use the same amount as called for with liquid. With no alcohol to evaporate, a stronger vanilla taste and more pungent aroma will result.

Desserts

130

Desserts

Apricot Rooibos Sorbet

Remember to prepare your ice cream maker ahead of time according to manufacturer's instructions.

1 Steep **Apricot Rooibos Tea** leaves in boiling water for 10 minutes. Strain tea leaves and stir in honey. Cool in refrigerator.

2 Stir in apricot juice. Chill.

Freeze in ice cream machine according to manufacturer's instructions.

Serves 8

2	cups boiling water
2	tbsp. **Apricot Rooibos Tea** leaves
¼	cup honey
2	cups apricot juice

Spiced Sugar Cookies

1 Preheat oven to 400°.

2 Wet Ingredients: Cream together the shortening and sugar. Beat in the eggs until well blended.

3 Dry Ingredients: In a separate bowl, mix together the flour, baking powder, salt and **Sweet Baking Spice**.

4 In a third large mixing bowl, blend the **Vanilla Powder** into the milk.

5 Add a small amount of the dry ingredients to the third mixing bowl and stir. Add a small amount of the wet ingredients to the third bowl and stir. Repeat until dry and wet ingredients are mixed well. Refrigerate, covered for 30 minutes.

6 Form the dough into 2 or 3 balls for handling ease. Roll on a floured board and cut into desired shapes with cookie cutters.

Place on an ungreased cookie sheet and bake for 7 to 10 minutes or until lightly browned. Cool on a rack. Frost with icing if desired.

Makes about 3 dozen cookies

1 ⅓	cup shortening
1 ¼	cup sugar
2	eggs
3 ½	cups flour
2	tsp. baking powder
1	tsp. salt
2 ½	tsp. **Sweet Baking Spice**
½	tsp. **Vanilla Powder**
¼	cup milk

Apricot Rooibos Sorbet

Lemon Drop Meringue Pie

Serves 8

1 favorite pie crust, previously baked according to package directions
½ cup lemon juice
6 egg yolks
¾ cup sugar plus ½ cup sugar
1 cup evaporated milk
1 tbsp. **Lemon Drop Rooibos Tea** leaves
1 tbsp. cornstarch
4 egg whites

1 Preheat the oven to broil.

2 Heat the lemon juice, egg yolks and the ¾ cup sugar in a small saucepan. Whisk frequently while this lemon curd comes to a simmer.

3 Add the evaporated milk and **Lemon Drop Rooibos Tea** leaves and simmer for approximately 4 minutes or until thick. Whisk in the cornstarch.

4 Spread this filling in the cooked pie crust.

5 With an electric mixer, beat the egg whites until they form soft peaks. Add the ½ cup sugar and continue beating until they form stiff peaks.

6 While the lemon filling is still hot, spread meringue on top.

7 Broil the pie for about 1 minute or until the meringue in perfectly browned. Watch very carefully at this stage, because if you leave it in for just a few extra seconds the meringue will burn.

8 Cool to room temperature and serve.

Warm Spiced Pecan Cakes

Makes 6 individual cakes

1 tbsp. butter, softened for ramekins (or substitute for a cupcake pan)

4 egg whites

6 tbsp. unsalted butter, melted

1 cup pecans

1 ½ cups powdered sugar

1 tsp. **Pumpkin Pie Spice**

⅓ cup flour

¼ tsp. salt

3 tbsp. honey

1 Preheat oven to 375°F.

2 Generously butter 6 ramekins with 1 tablespoon butter.

3 Separate the four egg whites from the yolk and set aside. Melt the 6 tablespoons of unsalted butter and set aside.

4 In a food processor, process the pecans until coarsely ground. Add the powdered sugar, **Pumpkin Pie Spice**, flour and salt. Process for 20 seconds.

5 Add egg whites and honey, blending to combine. With the food processor running, add the melted butter and process just to combine.

6 Distribute batter equally among the ramekins and bake for 25 to 35 minutes or until golden brown on top.

7 Press a pecan half into the top of each cake.

Cool on a wire rack for 5 minutes. Serve warm with vanilla ice cream if desired.

Lychee Rose Raspberry Gelatin

Serves 6

2 ½ cups water
½ cup sugar
3 tbsp. **Lychee Rose Black Tea** leaves
1 package gelatin (2 ½ tsp.)
1 tbsp. lemon juice
2 cups fresh raspberries

Random Tip#27

Sweet Dishes: To add a little extra flavor to any sweet dish, try adding a pinch of **Cinnamon**, **Nutmeg**, **Cloves** and/or **Allspice**.

1 In a small saucepan, heat the water and sugar to boiling.

2 Stir in the **Lychee Rose Black Tea** leaves, remove from heat, and cover. Let steep for 5 minutes and strain out the tea leaves.

3 Place the gelatin in a small bowl. Add ¼ cup of the hot tea liquid and let sit for 3 minutes or until the gelatin is dissolved.

4 Stir the gelatin into the hot tea and allow to slightly cool. Stir in the lemon juice.

5 Divide the raspberries evenly between 6 glasses.

6 Pour the cooled liquid overtop of the raspberries and refrigerate for several hours or until the gelatin has thickened.

Serve cold.

Chili Chocolate Brownies

Makes about 4 dozen

6 tbsp. butter

3 oz bittersweet chocolate

4 eggs

2 tsp. vanilla extract

1 ¾ cups sugar

½ cup flour

¼ cup **Spicy Chili Hot Chocolate Mix**

1 Preheat the oven to 350°F.

2 Grease a 9x13 inch baking pan.

3 Place the butter and chocolate in a small glass mixing bowl. Microwave to melt, being careful not to overheat.

4 Stir the butter and chocolate together and then beat in the eggs and vanilla.

5 Add the sugar, flour, **Spicy Chili Hot Chocolate** and stir to combine. Pour the batter into the prepared baking pan.

6 Bake the brownies for about 25 minutes or until a toothpick inserted in the middle comes out mostly clean (it can be a bit oily).

Cool on a rack before serving.

Mandarin Jasmine White Chocolate Mousse

1 Steep the **Mandarin Jasmine Pearl Tea** in the boiling water, covered, for 8 minutes.

2 Strain, pressing as much tea out as possible.

3 Melt the chocolate with about half the tea in a double boiler or in the microwave until just barely melted. Stir and set aside.

4 Very gently, over low heat or the top of a double boiler, heat the rest of the tea with the egg yolks, whisking frequently at first and constantly as it starts to warm, for 5 to 10 minutes.

5 When the mixture has warmed and become thick, foamy, and almost custardy, scrape the melted chocolate into the yolk mixture with a rubber spatula and whisk to combine.

6 Set aside to cool for a few minutes.

Serves 8-10

- 2 tbsp. **Mandarin Jasmine Pearl Tea**
- ½ cup water, boiling
- 7 oz high quality white chocolate
- 6 eggs, separated and at room temperature
- 2 cups heavy whipping cream, chilled
- ¼ tsp. **Cream of Tartar**
- ¼ cup plus 2 tbsp. sugar

  Mandarin segments (or another fruit of your choice) and mint sprigs, optional

7 In a medium to large mixing bowl, whip the cream until light and fluffy, mixing in 2 tablespoons of sugar near the end.

8 Gently fold in the chocolate and yolk mixture.

9 In another large mixing bowl, beat the egg whites with the **Cream of Tartar** until they reach soft peaks, sprinkling in the remaining ¼ cup sugar near the end. The whites should appear shiny and the bubbles should be very small. When you slowly lift the beater from the bowl, the whites should form a peak which holds its shape for the most part while folding over at the top.

10 Gently fold the cream and chocolate into the egg whites.

11 Divide among individual serving glasses or ramekins and chill in the refrigerator for a few hours or until ready to serve (they last a few days covered and refrigerated).

When ready to serve, garnish with the mandarin segments and perhaps a sprig of mint.

Ginger Pound Cake 🎀

Recipe Contest Winner!
Maryon from Lakeland, FL

Makes 16 servings

¼ cup plus 2 tbsp. margarine, softened

⅔ cups granulated sugar

4 egg whites

2 cups cake flour (or substitute 2 cups minus 4 tbsp. all-purpose flour)

¾ tsp. baking soda

¼ tsp. salt

1 tsp. **Ground Ginger**

¼ cup **Candied Ginger**, finely chopped

1 tbsp. ginger root, peeled and finely minced

1 8oz container low-fat lemon yogurt

2 tsp. **Vanilla Powder**

1 Preheat oven to 350°F.

2 Coat an 8 ½ x 4 ½ x 3 loaf pan with cooking spray. Dust pan with 1 teaspoon flour and set aside.

3 In a medium mixing bowl, beat margarine at medium speed until creamy. Gradually add sugar, beating well after each addition. Add egg whites and beat for 4 minutes.

4 In a separate mixing bowl, combine flour, baking soda, salt and **Ground Ginger**. Add this to margarine mixture alternately with yogurt, beginning and ending with flour mixture. Mix well after each addition.

5 Stir in **Candied Ginger**, ginger root and **Vanilla Powder**.

6 Pour batter into prepared pan and bake for 55 to 60 minutes or until a wooden pick inserted near center comes out clean.

7 Cool in pan on a wire rack for 10 minutes. Remove from pan and let cool completely on a wire rack.

Variation: if lemon yogurt is not available, use plain low-fat yogurt and add ⅛ tsp. **Lemon Flavoring** along with the **Vanilla Powder**.

Random Tip#28

Cinnamon Sugar: Make your own mix by combining: 7/8 cup granulated sugar + 2 tbsp. **Ground Cinnamon**. Keep in a shaker container.

Desserts

Cinnamon-Orange Trifle

Cardamom Rice Pudding

Serves 8

4 cups whole or 2% milk
½ cup long grain white rice
8 **Cardamom Seeds, Whole/Green**
½ cup sugar
1 tsp. cornstarch
Optional: ½ cup slivered almonds or chopped pistachios, ¼ cup raisins or currants
Optional: **Ground Cinnamon**

1 Heat the milk, rice, **Cardamom Seeds**, sugar and cornstarch in a medium saucepan over medium-high heat. If using, add the nuts and fruit at the same time.

2 When the mixture begins to boil, reduce the heat to medium-low and simmer uncovered for 25 to 35 minutes, stirring often.

3 Pudding is done when it has thickened and the rice is very soft (though it will thicken more as it cools).

4 Remove the **Cardamom Seeds** before cooling.

Serve warm or at room temperature. Garnish with **Ground Cinnamon**, if desired.

Cinnamon-Orange Trifle

Serves 8

- 4 cups whole milk
- 2 tbsp. **MarketSpice Cinnamon-Orange Black Tea** leaves
- 6 egg yolks
- 2 tbsp. cornstarch
- ½ cup sugar
- ¾ cup blackberry jam
- 1 angel food cake, cut or torn into 1" pieces (substitute ladyfingers or pound cake)
- 4 cups mixed berries

1 Heat the milk in a medium saucepan over medium heat, stirring almost constantly until it begins to simmer.

2 Remove from heat and add the **MarketSpice Cinnamon-Orange Black Tea**. Cover and steep for 10 minutes. Strain out the tea leaves.

3 In a medium bowl, whisk together the egg yolks, cornstarch, sugar and ½ cup of the milk and tea mixture. Continue adding more milk until the mixture is very thin.

4 Return the pot of the remaining milk to medium heat. Once it begins to simmer, slowly pour in the egg mixture while whisking constantly. Immediately reduce the heat to medium-low and cook, stirring constantly until the custard begins to thicken. It should be thick enough to coat a wooden spoon.

5 Remove from heat, transfer to a mixing bowl and lay plastic wrap directly on the surface of the custard. Allow to cool for at least 30 minutes. At this point, the custard can be kept for a day or two in the refrigerator.

6 For serving, you will want either a trifle dish, a clear serving bowl with straight sides or individual glasses.

7 In the bottom, add a layer of angel food cake. Spread with a layer of jam. Top that with 1 cup of berries and evenly pour on a third of the custard sauce. Repeat three times and top with the remaining berries.

8 Refrigerate for at least 2 hours before serving.

Random Tip#29

Herb/Spice Storage: Storing in the fridge is not recommended because of the humid environment. To keep large quantities fresh, store them in the freezer in tightly sealed containers.

Earl Grey Chocolate Cake

1 Preheat oven to 350°F. Butter and flour a round 8-inch cake pan (it should be at least 1 ½ inches deep. If it is shallower, go with a 9-inch cake pan).

2 In a small bowl or measuring cup, combine the boiling water and the **Earl Grey Black Tea**. Cover with foil and let steep for 7 minutes or until the tea is very strong.

3 Strain the leaves out, pushing as much liquid out of them as possible. Measure out 5 tablespoons of the tea into the bowl of a double boiler over simmering water and add the chocolate.

4 Stir until the chocolate is melted. Alternatively, you can melt the chocolate with the tea in a microwave, being careful not to let it go too long to avoid overcooking.

5 In a large mixing bowl, use an electric beater to cream the butter and ⅔ cup of the sugar. It should take about 2 minutes to reach a truly creamy consistency. Beat in the egg yolks until the mixture is well blended.

6 In a separate medium mixing bowl, beat the egg whites with the **Cream of Tartar** and salt until they reach soft peaks. Add the remaining tablespoon of sugar and continue to beat until the whites form stiff peaks.

7 Using a rubber spatula, fold the melted chocolate into the butter and sugar mixture. When the chocolate is fully incorporated, add the ground almonds and stir to combine.

8 Lighten the mixture by stirring in ¼ of the beaten egg whites. Add half the flour and fold to combine. Add another ¼ of egg whites, folding lightly to combine and repeat with the remaining flour and the remaining whites.

9 Turn the batter into the prepared cake pan, pushing the batter up around the edges with the rubber spatula.

Serves 8

½ cup boiling water

2 tbsp. **Earl Grey Black Tea** leaves

4 oz high quality semisweet chocolate, chopped

1 stick unsalted butter, softened

⅔ cup plus 1 tbsp. sugar

3 eggs, separated

Scant ¼ tsp. **Cream of Tartar**

Pinch of salt

⅓ cup finely ground almonds

½ cup cake flour (or substitute ½ cup minus 1 tbsp. all-purpose flour)

Sliced almonds and powdered sugar, for garnish

10 Bake the cake for 25 minutes or until it is puffy and a toothpick inserted one inch from the edge comes out clean and the center is almost set (it should still move a little bit when shaken).

11 Cool the cake on a wire rack for 15 minutes before running a sharp knife around the edge to loosen. Reverse the cake onto a serving plate.

If you want to ice it, it must cool for at least an hour before icing. Otherwise, you may serve it warm with only a dusting of powdered sugar and a few sliced almonds for garnish.

Desserts

MarketSpice Chocolate Pots de Crème

Serves 8

1   cup cream, hot

1 ½ cups whole milk, hot

6   egg yolks

3   oz **MarketSpice Cinnamon-Orange Hot Chocolate Mix** (or substitute **Mint Hot Chocolate Mix or Raspberry Hot Chocolate Mix**)

Boiling water

Whipped cream, optional

1 Preheat the oven to 325°F.

2 In a small mixing bowl, blend the cream, milk and egg yolks.

3 Place the **MarketSpice Cinnamon-Orange Hot Chocolate Mix** in a large bowl and while whisking, gradually add the milk and egg mixture.

4 Place 8 ramekins in a baking pan and distribute the batter evenly between the ramekins.

5 Pour the boiling water in the baking pan, avoiding splashing the pots de crème.

6 Bake for 20 minutes or until the pots de crème wobble slightly when shaken but are no longer liquid.

Let cool slightly outside the water bath and serve warm with a spoonful of whipped cream if desired.

Salted Truffles

Makes approximately 25 truffles

6   oz high quality semisweet chocolate,
     chopped
⅓   cup cream
⅓   cup **Pernigotti Cocoa**
2   tbsp. **Himalayan Pink Salt**, crushed in a
     mortar and pestle

1 Place the chocolate in a small glass mixing bowl.

2 Heat the cream to nearly boiling in a small saucepan over medium heat and pour over the chocolate. Allow to sit for 2 minutes and then stir to combine.

3 If the chocolate is not fully melted, microwave in increments of 15 seconds until it completely melts when stirred.

4 Once the chocolate and cream are well combined, set aside to cool completely. This should take at least 2 hours but it's easiest to leave it overnight.

5 With a small teaspoon or melon baller, scoop the chocolate into small balls. With your hands and rubber gloves if available, roll each ball into nearly-perfect rounds.

6 Roll each one in the **Pernigotti Cocoa** to coat and then press a pinch of **Himalayan Pink Salt** on the top.

Chill in the refrigerator before serving.

Peach & Blueberry Crisp with Spiced Hazelnut Crumble

1 In a large mixing bowl combine flour, brown sugar, oats, hazelnuts and **Pumpkin Pie Spice**. Stir together until well mixed.

2 Add the butter and using an electric mixer, blend until no piece of butter is larger than a grain of rice. Set aside.

Part 1: Crumble Layer

⅓ cup flour

⅓ cup brown sugar

⅓ cup oats

½ cup hazelnuts, finely chopped

1 tbsp. **Pumpkin Pie Spice**

5 tbsp. butter, softened and cut into ½ inch cubes

1 Preheat oven to 375°F.

2 In a large bowl toss together the peaches, blueberries, tapioca, sugar and lemon juice. Transfer to a 9" square cake or pie pan.

3 Cover with the crumble and bake for 25 to 35 minutes, or until the topping is browned and the filling bubbles up on the edges.

4 Cool on a wire rack for 10 minutes.

Part 2 - Fruit Layer
Serves 10

4 cups sliced peaches (blanched and peeled, optional)

1 ½ cups blueberries

½ cup small pearl tapioca

½ cup sugar

1 tbsp. lemon juice

Serve warm or at room temperature. Add whip cream if desired.

Random Tip#30
Toasting Spices: Toasting whole spices in a dry skillet over medium heat before grinding will bring out even more flavor. Be careful not to burn.

Coriander Shortbread Cookies

Makes approximately 40 cookies

1 tbsp. **Coriander Seeds**

½ cup sugar

2 cups flour

2 sticks unsalted butter, chilled and in ½
inch cubes

1 Preheat the oven to 300°F.

2 Place the **Coriander Seeds**, sugar and flour in a food processor and blend for at least one minute in order to grind the coriander (don't worry if it isn't fully ground).

3 Add the butter and pulse until the dough comes together, about 20 seconds. (If a food processor isn't available substitute seeds for **Ground Coriander**).

4 Place the dough on a piece of parchment paper on top of a flat surface, form the dough into a ball and cover with another sheet of parchment paper.

5 With a rolling pin, roll the dough out to ¼ inch thick. Remove the top sheet of parchment paper and cut into the dough ½ inch by 2 inch cookies or use a cookie cutter to form your desired cookie shape, keeping in mind that the cookies will spread out slightly when baking.

6 Bake on an ungreased cookie sheet for 20 to 30 minutes or until dry and slightly darker beige.

Let cool for at least 15 minutes before serving.

Cherry Almond Clafoutis

1 Preheat the oven to 400°F.

2 Use the butter to grease an 8 or 9 inch round glass pie pan. Arrange the pitted cherries evenly in the pie pan.

3 Heat the milk in a small saucepan until it begins to bubble.

4 Remove from heat, add the **Cherry Almond Black Tea** leaves, cover and steep for 5 minutes.

5 Strain the tea leaves and add additional milk as needed to make 1 cup.

6 In a medium mixing bowl, stir together the flour and sugar.

7 Add the milk/tea mixture and the eggs, then beat to combine.

8 Pour this batter over the cherries and bake for 25 to 30 minutes or until the Clafouti is slightly puffed and beginning to brown.

9 Remove from the oven, dust with powdered sugar, slice and serve immediately. This Clafoutis is particularly good served with vanilla ice cream.

Serves 6 to 8

1	tbsp. butter, softened
2	cups pitted cherries
1	cup whole milk
2	tbsp. **Cherry Almond Black Tea** leaves
¾	cup flour
½	cup sugar
2	eggs
	Powdered sugar for serving

Desserts

Huckleberry Ice Cream with Cinnamon Berries

Remember to prepare your ice cream maker ahead of time according to manufacturer's instructions.

1 Bring the milk and sugar to a simmer in a small saucepan.

2 Add the **Huckleberry Crème Black Tea** leaves, cover and remove from heat. Let steep for 5 minutes and then strain. Cool in the refrigerator.

3 Whisk in the sour cream. Freeze in an ice cream machine, following manufacturer's instructions.

Put in freezer until serving time.

Part 1 - Ice Cream:
Serves 6

2   cups whole milk
1   cup sugar
2   tbsp. **Huckleberry Crème Black Tea** leaves
2   cups low-fat sour cream

1 In a small saucepan, bring the berries, **Ground Cinnamon**, water and ¼ cup sugar to a gentle simmer over low heat.

2 Simmer for 1 minute, or until many of the berries pop. Remove from heat.

To serve: Top each scoop of ice cream with a spoonful of warm berries.

Part 2 - Warm Berries:

1   pint mixed berries
    A pinch of **Ground Cinnamon**
2   tbsp. water
¼   cup sugar

Random Tip#31
Smoothies, Shakes & Ice Cream: Stir 1 tsp. **Matcha Powder** into any smoothie, shake or ice cream for added antioxidants.

Desserts

BEVERAGES

Raspberry Smash

4 tbsp. **Raspberry Splash Rooibos Tea** leaves

1 cup water

1 cup sugar

Vodka, Rum or spirit of choice

Club Soda

Several limes (muddled)

1 Steep the **Raspberry Splash Rooibos Tea** leaves in the boiling water for 5 to 8 minutes. Strain out the tea leaves.

2 Make a simple syrup by stirring sugar into the tea in a small saucepan over low heat until sugar dissolves. Allow to cool in refrigerator for at least 30 minutes.

3 Mix or shake 2 shots of the syrup, 1 to 2 shots of spirit, ½ cup of club soda and ½ of a muddled lime.

Pour over ice and serve cold.

Grapefruit Peony Iced Tea

2 tbs. **White Peony Tea** leaves
4 cups boiling water
¼ cup honey
1 cup grapefruit juice

1 Steep the **White Peony Tea** in the boiling water for 4 minutes. Strain out the tea leaves.

2 Stir in the honey to dissolve. Chill the tea mixture in the refrigerator.

3 When the tea is cool and you are ready to serve, stir in the grapefruit juice and serve over ice.

Egg Nog Latte

2 cups whole or 2% milk
1 tbsp. **Egg Nog Black Tea** leaves
Sugar, optional
Cinnamon Sticks for garnish

1 Heat the milk to almost boiling in a small saucepan.

2 Add the **Egg Nog Black Tea** and steep, covered for 2 minutes.

3 Strain and pour into two mugs.

4 Serve, using a cinnamon stick to stir if desired.

Hibiscus Ginger Ale ✨

2 tbsp. **Hibiscus Herbal Tea** leaves

1 tsp. **Ground Ginger**

4 cups boiling water

½ cup sugar

1 quart club soda or sparkling water (about 4 cups)

1 Steep the **Hibiscus Herbal Tea** leaves and **Ground Ginger** in the boiling water for 5 to 10 minutes. (The longer it steeps, the more ginger flavor comes through.) Strain the tea leaves.

2 Stir in the sugar to dissolve. Chill the tea mixture in the refrigerator.

3 When the tea is cool and you are ready to serve, stir in the club soda or sparkling water.

Spicy Chai with Spirits

4 cups whole milk

¼ cup honey

2 tbsp. **Spicy Seattle Chai Black Tea** leaves

Kahlua, Irish Cream or spirit of choice

1 In a medium saucepan, heat milk, honey and **Spicy Seattle Chai Black Tea**, stirring constantly.

2 Remove from heat before it boils, strain out tea leaves and serve in mugs.

3 Add 1 to 2 shots of spirits as desired.

Green Tea Latte

2 cups whole or 2% milk
2 tbsp. brown sugar
1 tbsp. **Gunpowder Green Tea** leaves

1 Heat the milk and brown sugar to almost boiling in a small saucepan, stirring to dissolve the sugar.

2 Add the **Gunpowder Green Tea** leaves and steep covered for 2 or 3 minutes, or until the flavor is as strong as desired.

3 Strain out the tea leaves and pour into two mugs.

Passion Fruit Lemon Cooler

4 cups boiling water
3 tbsp. **Passion Fruit Black Tea** leaves
⅓ cup honey
¼ cup lemon juice
4 cups cold water
Ice cubes
Garnish: lemon peel or mint (optional)

1 Boil the 4 cups of water and remove from heat. Add the **Passion Fruit Black Tea** leaves and steep covered for 4 minutes. Strain the tea leaves.

2 Stir in the honey to dissolve. Cool to room temperature and stir in the lemon juice and water.

3 Chill and serve over ice. Garnish with lemon peel or mint, if desired.

Beverages

Cucumber Mint Limeade

Part 1 – Cucumber Juice:

1 English cucumber, sliced into 1 inch segments
¼ cup water

1 In a blender, puree the cucumber with the water for about 30 seconds or until completely smooth.

2 Strain out the pulp using a fine strainer or cheesecloth and reserve.

This juice will last a few days in the refrigerator.

Part 2 – Cucumber Mint Limeade:
Makes 6 cups

4 cups water
2 tbsp. **Spearmint Herbal Tea** leaves
6 tbsp. sugar
1 cup Cucumber Juice, see Part 1
1 cup lime juice
Optional: 1 oz vodka mixed with each glass of Cucumber Mint Limeade
Garnish: fresh mint

1 Bring water to a boil and remove from heat. Steep the **Spearmint Herbal Tea** leaves in the water for 6 minutes. Strain out the tea leaves.

2 Stir in the sugar to dissolve.

3 Chill thoroughly in the refrigerator and stir in the Cucumber Juice and lime juice.

4 Serve over ice and garnish with fresh mint.

If you want to make this drink a cocktail, shake 1 oz of vodka with ½ a cup of the drink mixture before serving over ice.

Random Tip#32

Spiking Hot Tea: Spiking iced tea is really common but spiking hot tea can be just as tasty. Some good combinations are: **Earl Grey** with Grand Marnier, **Assam** with Apricot Brandy, any plain **White Tea** with Elderberry flower liqueur, **Green Tea** with ginger liqueur, etc.
Just a splash is sufficient.

Beverages

Assam Orange Soda

4 cups boiling water

2 tbsp. **Assam Black Tea** leaves

¼ cup honey

4 cups fresh squeezed orange juice

1 quart club soda or sparkling water

1 Steep the **Assam Black Tea** leaves in the boiling water for 5 minutes.

2 Strain tea leaves and stir in honey. Cool in refrigerator.

3 When ready to serve, stir in the club soda or sparkling water and orange juice. Serve cold.

Oolong White Grape Juice

4   cups water
2   tbsp. **Jade Spring Oolong Tea** leaves
4   cups white grape juice
    Ice cubes

1 Bring 4 cups of water to a boil. Remove from heat and add the **Jade Spring Oolong Tea** leaves. Steep the tea for 7 minutes. Strain out the tea leaves. Chill with the ice cubes.

2 Stir in the white grape juice and chill thoroughly in the refrigerator.

3 Serve over ice and garnish with fresh mint, if desired.

Fancy Hot Chocolate

6 tbsp. **Hot Chocolate Mix**
    (MarketSpice Cinnamon-Orange, Mint,
    Raspberry, Vanilla or Spicy Chile)
4 cups whole milk
    Mini marshmallows
    Kahlua, Irish Cream or spirit of choice

1 In a medium saucepan, bring milk to a slow simmer over low heat. Add almost all of the 6 tablespoons of **Hot Chocolate Mix**, leaving a teaspoon or so for garnish.

2 Whisk until well blended and pour into mugs.

3 Add 1 to 2 shots of spirits.

4 Top with mini marshmallows and remaining **Hot Chocolate Mix**.

Serve immediately.

Chai Apple Cider

4 cups apple cider or apple juice
2 tbsp. **Market Chai Black Tea** leaves

1 Heat the cider in a small saucepan until bubbles appear.

2 Remove from heat and add the **Market Chai Black Tea** leaves, steep for 4 minutes and strain.

Serve hot or cold.

Random Tip#33

Cooking with Tea Leaves: Chop Green or African RedBush tea leaves and combine with spices to coat chicken, fish or steak before cooking.

Honey Rose Lassi

1½ cups boiling water
1 tbsp. **Rosebuds & Petals**
¼ cup honey
1 ½ cups plain yogurt (**Not** non-fat)

1 Remove boiling water from heat source. In medium, heat-resistant bowl add boiling water and **Rosebuds & Petals**. Let steep for approximately 5 minutes.

2 Strain petals and stir in the honey to liquid and allow to dissolve. Refrigerate until fully cool.

3 Stir in the yogurt and serve over ice if desired.

Black Currant Sangria

1 cup boiling water
½ cup sugar
2 tbsp. **Black Currant Black Tea** leaves
1 bottle dry rosé wine
1 pint of strawberries, sliced
1 lemon, very thinly sliced in rounds
2 tangerines, sections separated
3 cups sparkling water

1 Combine the water and sugar in a small saucepan and bring to a boil. Remove from heat.

2 Add the **Black Currant Black Tea** leaves and let steep for 5 minutes. Strain the tea leaves and cool for 30 minutes in the fridge.

3 Combine the berries and fruit in a large clear pitcher and add the sugar/tea mixture and wine.

4 Chill for at least one hour and up to 2 days.

5 Stir in the sparkling water right before serving.

Simple Bloody Mary

3 oz vodka (2 shots)
1 ¼ cup tomato juice
2 tbsp. lemon juice
2 tsp. **Bloody Mary Mix**
  Ice
2 slices lemon
2 4" sticks of celery
2 4" carrot slices

1 In a cocktail shaker, shake together the vodka, tomato juice, lemon juice and **Bloody Mary Mix**. Variation: whisk them together in a small bowl if a cocktail shaker is unavailable.

2 Fill two highball glasses with ice, pouring the Bloody Mary over the ice.

3 Garnish each one with a celery stick, a slice of carrot and a slice of lemon. Serve cold.

Peach Iced Tea

2 tbsp. **<u>Assam Black Tea</u>** leaves or
<u>Northwest Breakfast Black Tea</u> leaves

4 cups boiling water

4 cups peach nectar

1 Steep the **<u>Assam Black Tea</u>** leaves in the boiling water for 4 minutes. Strain out the leaves. Chill the tea in the refrigerator.

2 When the tea is cool and you are ready to serve, stir in the peach juice and serve over ice.

Variation: substitute your favorite fruit nectar or any preferred juice to tailor this recipe to your preferences.

Random Tip#34

Herb, Spice & Dry Tea Shelf Life: As a general rule, herbs, ground spices and dry tea, will retain their best flavor for 1 year. Whole spices may last for 3 to 5 years. Teas containing flavoring oils last approximately 6 months.

Pineapple Ginger Agua Fresca

4 cups boiling water
3 tbsp. **Ginger Lemon Herbal Tea** leaves
3 tbsp. **Honey Granules**
1 20oz can of Pineapple chunks in juice

1 Boil the water, remove from heat and steep the **Ginger Lemon Herbal Tea** leaves covered for 15 minutes. Strain out the tea leaves.

2 Stir in the **Honey Granules** until dissolved. Refrigerate to chill.

3 Meanwhile, put the can of pineapple with the juice in a blender and puree until smooth. Strain the pineapple, stirring the part in the strainer frequently to allow the maximum amount of juice to come through.

4 Combine the tea and the pineapple puree. Garnish with mint or a pineapple wedge and serve over ice.

Variation: For an alcoholic version of this drink, stir one shot of rum with each cup of juice.

Southern Sweet Tea

2 tbsp. **Keemun Black Tea** leaves
4 cups boiling water
Pinch of baking soda
1 cup sugar
1 tray of ice cubes
Lemon slice, for garnish

1 Steep the **Keemun Black Tea** leaves in the boiling water for 4 minutes. Strain out the tea leaves.

2 Stir in the baking soda and sugar to dissolve.

3 Chill with the ice cubes to speed up the process and then refrigerate until cold.

4 Serve over ice and garnish with a slice of lemon.

Cinnamon-Orange Sweet Tea (lower calorie):

Prepare the same way as the above recipe, substituting **MarketSpice Cinnamon-Orange Black Tea** leaves for the **Keemun Black Tea** leaves, and using only ¼ cup sugar (or to taste).

Ingredients Glossary

#

13th Wonder: Fine Sea Salt, Garlic, Onion & Pepper Black

9-Spice Rice Seasoning: Basil, Garlic, Marjoram, Paprika Sweet, Pepper Black, Rosemary & Thyme

A

Apricot Rooibos Tea: African RedBush Tea, Apricot Flavoring (N&A) & Peach Flavoring (N&A)

Apricot Rooibos

B

Barbeque Spice SF: Allspice, Basil, Bayleaves, Brown Sugar, Celery Seed, Chili Powder SF, Cinnamon, Cloves, Coriander, Cumin, Fructose, Garlic, Garlic Powder, Ginger, Liquid Smoke, Marjoram, Mustard Powder Hot & Mild, Nutmeg, Onion, Onion Powder, Oregano, Paprika Hot, Parsley, Pepper Black, Rosemary, Sage, Savory, Spearmint, Star Anise & Thyme

Beaumonde: Celery Seed, Dextrose, Fine Sea Salt & Onion

Berbere (Ethiopian All-Purpose): Allspice, Cayenne 50 SHU, Cloves, Coriander, Fenugreek, Ginger, Mace, Onion, Paprika Spanish, Sel Gris de Guerande Salt & Tellicherry Peppercorns

Black Currant Tea: Hunan Tea & Black Currant Flavoring (N&A)

Blackened Redfish SF: Cayenne 25 SHU, Garlic, Onion, Oregano, Paprika Sweet, Pepper Black, Pepper White & Thyme

Bombay Mix

Bleu Cheese Herb Dressing Mix: Celery Salt, Fine Sea Salt, Garlic, Paprika Sweet & Pepper Black

Bloody Mary Mix: Cayenne 25 SHU, Celery Salt, Celery Seed, Paprika Spanish, Pepper Black & Worcestershire Powder

Bombay Mix: Cayenne 25 SHU, Cloves, Coriander, Cumin, Curry Powder Regular, Garlic, Onion, Sesame Seeds & Turmeric

Bouquet Garni SF: Basil, Dill Weed, Marjoram, Oregano, Rosemary, Sage, Savory, Tarragon & Thyme

Buttermilk Herb Dressing Mix: Basil, Garlic, Onion, Oregano, Parsley & Rosemary

C

Cajun Seasoning: Cayenne 100 SHU, Garlic, Mustard Powder Hot, Pepper Black & Pepper White

Carne Asada: Cilantro, Cumin, Lime Juice Powder, Pepper Black & Yakima Applewood Smoked Salt

Chai Mix: Cardamom Decorticated, Cinnamon Chips, Cloves, Coriander, Ginger, Nutmeg & Orange Peel Chopped

Cherry Almond Tea: Hunan Tea, Almond Flavoring (A) & Wild Cherry Flavoring (N&A)

Chile Lime Rub: Chili Pepper Chipotle, Chili Powder New Mexican, Cilantro, Cumin, Garlic, Lime Juice Powder & Oregano

Chinese 5-Spice: Allspice, Cinnamon, Coriander, Ginger & Star Anise

Carne Asada

Country Herb Blend SF

Chutney Mix: Cayenne 25 SHU, Chili Powder SF, Cinnamon, Cloves, Coriander, Cumin, Ginger & Nutmeg

Coleslaw Spice: Celery Seed, Mustard Powder Mild, Paprika Sweet & Pepper White

Country Herb Blend w/ Salt: Dextrose, Dill Weed, Garlic, Lemon Crystals, MSG, Onion, Onion Salt, Paprika Hot, Paprika Sweet, Parsley, Poppy Seeds & Sesame Seeds

Country Herb Blend SF: Dill Weed, Garlic, Garlic Powder, Onion, Onion Powder, Parsley, Paprika Sweet, Poppy Seeds & Sesame Seeds

Creamy Herb Dressing Mix: Basil, Chervil, Dill Weed, Garlic, Oregano, Parsley, Pepper White, Rosemary, Spearmint & Thyme

E

Earl Grey Tea: Hunan Tea & Bergamot Flavoring (N&A)

Egg Nog Tea: Assam Tea, Ceylon Tea, Darjeeling Tea, Cinnamon Chips, Nutmeg & Egg Nog Flavoring (N&A)

F

Fettuccini Spice Blend: Oregano, Basil, Rosemary, Marjoram, Savory & Thyme

Fine Herbs: Chervil, Chives, Marjoram, Parsley, Savory, Tarragon & Thyme

French Salad Dressing Mix: Garlic, Mustard Powder Mild, Paprika Sweet & Pepper White

G

Game Hen Blend: Flake Salt, Garlic, Onion, Oregano, Paprika Sweet & Pepper Black

Ginger Lemon Tea: Honeybush, Lemon Grass, Lemon Peel Chopped, Lemon Peel Granulated & Ginger

Greek Seasoning SF: Garlic, Lemon Peel Granulated, Oregano & Pepper Black

Green Herb Seafood Seasoning SF: Celery Seed, Dill Weed, Garlic, Lemon Pepper Spicy, Marjoram, Nutmeg, Onion, Parsley Flakes, Pepper White & Tarragon

Green Magic Dressing Mix: Dextrose, Fine Sea Salt, Parsley, MSG & Onion

Ginger Lemon Tea

H

Harissa Seasoning: Cayenne 25 SHU, Chili Powder New Mexican, Coriander, Cumin, Crushed Red Peppers, Fine Sea Salt, Garlic, Paprika Sweet & Spearmint

Healthy Heart Seasoning SF: Cayenne 50 SHU, Chervil, Coriander, Dill Weed, Fennel Seed, Garlic, Onion & Paprika Sweet

Herbs de Provence: Basil, Chervil, Lavender Flowers, Oregano, Parsley Flake, Rosemary, Savory, Tarragon & Thyme

Honey Mustard Dressing Mix: Celery Seed, Fine Sea Salt, Mustard Powder Mild, Paprika Sweet & Pepper White

Huckleberry Crème Tea: Hunan Tea & Huckleberry Crème Flavoring (N&A)

Herbs de Provence

I

Iranian Rice Blend: Chives, Cilantro, Dill Weed & Parsley

Italian Sausage Mix: Allspice, Crushed Red Peppers, Fennel Seed, Garlic, Pepper Black & Thyme

Italian Seasoning, Ground: Crushed Red Peppers, Oregano, Basil, Rosemary, Marjoram, Savory & Thyme

Italian Vinaigrette Dressing Mix: Basil, Dextrose, Fine Sea Salt, Garlic, Mustard Powder Mild, Onion, Oregano, Paprika Sweet & Pepper Black

J

Jamaican Jerk Seasoning: Habanero, Onion, Pepper Black, Pepper White, Salt, Sugar, Thyme, Vegetable Oil & spices

Japanese 7-Spice: Cayenne 50 SHU, Crushed Red Peppers, Fine Sea Salt, Lemon Peel Chopped, Mustard Seed Dark, Orange Peel Chopped, Poppy Seeds & Sesame Seed Black

K

Kashmiri Masala: Cardamom Ground, Cinnamon, Cloves, Cumin, Mace & Pepper Black

L

Japanese 7-Spice

Lemon Drop Rooibos Tea: African RedBush Tea, Lemon Peel Chopped, Peppermint Leaves & Lemon Flavoring (N)

Lychee Rose Tea: Lychee Tea, Rosebuds & Rose Petals

M

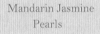
Mandarin Jasmine Pearls

Mandarin Jasmine Pearl Tea: Dragon Phoenix Pearl Tea, Orange Peel Chopped & Mandarin Flavoring (N)

Marinara Blend: Basil, Garlic, Oregano, Marjoram, Crushed Red Peppers, Rosemary, Savory & Thyme

Market Chai Tea: Assam Tea, Vanilla Tea, Cardamom Decorticated, Cinnamon Chips, Cloves, Coriander Seeds, Ginger, Nutmeg & Orange Peel Chopped

Market Seasoning Natural w/ Salt: Celery Seed, Cumin, Fine Sea Salt, Garlic, Mustard Powder Mild, Onion, Oregano, Paprika Sweet, Pepper Black & Turmeric

Market Chai Tea

Market Seasoning w/ Salt: Celery Seed, Cumin, Dextrose, Fine Sea Salt, Garlic, MSG, Mustard Powder Hot, Onion, Oregano, Paprika Sweet, Pepper Black & Turmeric

MarketSpice Cinnamon-Orange Hot Chocolate: Cinnamon, Cloves, Granulated Sugar, Pernigotti Cocoa & Orange Flavoring (N)

MarketSpice Cinnamon-Orange Tea: Hunan Tea, Orange Peel, Cloves, Cinnamon Flavoring (A) & Orange Flavoring (N)

Mexicali Mix: Chili Powder SF, Cilantro, Crushed Red Peppers, Cumin, Garlic, Onion, Oregano, Paprika Sweet & Thyme

Mint Hot Chocolate: Granulated Sugar, Pernigotti Cocoa & Peppermint Flavoring (N)

N

Northwest Breakfast Tea: Ceylon Tea & Darjeeling Tea

P

Panch Phoron

Panch Phoron: Cumin Seed, Fennel Seed, Fenugreek, Mustard Seed Dark & Nigella Seeds

Parmesan Dressing Mix: Celery Seed, Dextrose, Fine Sea Salt, Garlic, Mustard Powder Mild, Paprika Sweet & Pepper Black

Passion Fruit Tea: Hunan Tea & Passion Fruit Flavoring (N&A)

Pickling Spice: Allspice, Anise Seed, Bayleaves, Celery Seed, Cinnamon Chips, Cloves, Coriander, Crushed Red Peppers, Cumin, Dill Seed, Fennel Seed, Mustard Seed Dark & Light, Pepper Black & White & Turmeric

Poultry Seasoning: Allspice, Basil, Bayleaves, Celery Seed, Cinnamon, Cloves, Cumin, Garlic, Garlic Powder, Nutmeg, Onion Powder, Oregano, Paprika Sweet, Parsley Ground, Pepper Black, Rosemary, Sage, Savory, Spearmint & Thyme

Pumpkin Pie Spice: Allspice, Cinnamon, Ginger & Nutmeg

Q

Quick & Easy BBQ Sauce Blend: Allspice, Basil, Bayleaves, Brown Sugar, Celery Seed, Chili Powder SF, Cinnamon, Cloves, Coriander, Crushed Red Peppers, Cumin, Fructose, Garlic Powder, Ginger, Liquid Smoke, Marjoram, Mustard Powder Hot, Mustard Powder Mild, Nutmeg, Onion Powder, Oregano, Paprika Hot, Parsley, Pepper Black, Rosemary, Sage, Savory, Spearmint, Star Anise & Thyme

Quick & Easy BBQ Sauce Blend

R

Ranchero Mix: Basil, Chives, Cilantro, Coriander, Crushed Red Peppers, Cumin, Garlic & Parsley

Ras el Hanout (Moroccan): Allspice, Cardamom Whole Green, Cayenne 50 SHU, Cinnamon, Cloves, Coriander, Cumin, Fennel Seed, Fine Sea Salt, Ginger, Mace, Paprika Sweet, Saffron, Tellicherry Peppercorns & Turmeric

Raspberry Hot Chocolate: Granulated Sugar, Pernigotti Cocoa & Raspberry Flavoring (N)

Raspberry Splash Tea: Green African RedBush Tea, Lemon Peel Chopped, Raspberry Flakes, Lemon Flavoring (N) & Raspberry Flavoring (N&A)

S

Salmon Rub: Brownulated Sugar, Celery Seed, Dextrose, Dill Weed, Fine Sea Salt, Garlic Pepper Ground, Lemon Pepper Ground, Onion & Paprika Smoked

Raspberry Splash Tea

Salsa Mix: Cayenne 25 SHU, Chili Pepper Ancho, Cilantro, Coriander, Crushed Red Peppers, Cumin, Fructose, Garlic, Onion & Oregano

Sausage Mix: Allspice, Basil, Bayleaves, Celery Seed, Cinnamon, Cloves, Cumin, Garlic, Garlic Powder, Ginger, Marjoram, Nutmeg, Onion, Onion Powder, Oregano, Paprika Sweet, Parsley Flakes, Parsley Ground, Pepper Black, Rosemary, Sage, Savory, Spearmint & Thyme

Savory Herb Blend SF: Basil, Marjoram, Oregano, Rosemary & Sage

Seafood Seasoning w/ Salt: Dextrose, Fine Sea Salt, Fructose, Garlic, Lemon Peel Powder, Onion, Oregano, Paprika Sweet, Parsley Flakes, Pepper Black, Sour Salt & Tarragon

Salsa Mix

Seafood Seasoning SF: Celery Seed, Dill Seed, Dill Weed, Garlic, Lemon Peel Powder, Mustard Powder Mild, Nutmeg, Onion, Paprika Sweet, Parsley Ground, Pepper Black, Pepper White, Sour Salt & Turmeric

Seasoned Salt: Fine Sea Salt, Fructose, Garlic, Onion, Oregano, Paprika Sweet, Pepper Black & Sour Salt

Smokey Meat Rub: Garlic, Onion, Paprika Smoked, Pepper Black, Worcestershire Powder & Yakima Applewood Smoked Salt

Spaghetti Sauce Mix SF: Basil, Fennel Seed, Garlic, Onion, Oregano & Parsley Flakes

Ingredients Glossary

Spicy Chile
Hot Chocolate

Spicy BBQ Sauce Blend: Allspice, Basil, Bayleaves, Brown Sugar, Cayenne 25 SHU, Celery Seed, Chili Pepper Ancho, Cinnamon, Cloves, Coriander, Crushed Red Peppers, Cumin, Fructose, Garlic, Ginger, Liquid Smoke, Marjoram, Mustard Powder Milk, Mustard Powder Hot, Nutmeg, Onion, Oregano, Paprika Hot, Parsley, Pepper Black, Rosemary, Sage, Savory, Spearmint & Star Anise

Spicy Chile Hot Chocolate: Cayenne 25 SHU, Cinnamon, Granulated Sugar, Pernigotti Cocoa & Vanilla Bean Granules

Spicy Lemon Pepper SF: Dill Seed, Lemon Peel Powder, Onion, Pepper Black, Pepper White, Turmeric & Sour Salt

Spicy Seattle Chai Tea: Hunan Tea, Assam Tea, Cardamom Whole Green, Cinnamon Chips, Ginger & Tellicherry Peppercorns

Sweet Baking Spice: Allspice, Cinnamon & Nutmeg

T

Taco Seasoning SF: Chili Powder SF, Cilantro, Coriander, Crushed Red Peppers, Cumin, Garlic & Oregano

Tandoori Masala: Cayenne 25 SHU, Coriander, Cumin, Garlic, Ginger, Mace, Paprika Smoked & Turmeric

Spicy Seattle Chai Tea

Texas BBQ Sauce Blend: Chili Powder SF, Garlic, Mustard Powder Mild, Paprika Hot & Pepper Black

Turkey Brine Mix: Rosemary, Sage, Savory & Thyme

V

Vanilla Hot Chocolate: Granulated Sugar, Pernigotti Cocoa & Vanilla Bean Granules

Veggie Chip Dip Mix: Celery Seed, Dextrose, Dill Weed, Fine Sea Salt, Onion & Parsley

Vindaloo Curry: Cayenne 50 SHU, Cinnamon, Cloves, Coriander, Cumin, Fine Sea Salt, Ginger, Mustard Powder Hot, Pepper Black & Turmeric

Y

Yogurt Dill Dressing Mix: Celery Seed, Dextrose, Fine Sea Salt, Garlic, Onion & Pepper Black

Z

Za'atar Blend: Fine Sea Salt, Oregano, Sesame Seeds Toasted, Sumac & Thyme

Veggie Chip Dip Mix

Terms Glossary

A

Agua Fresca: a fruit drink served cold traditionally made of a fruit juice, water and sugar mixture

Albondigas: meatballs made of chicken, shrimp, beef or pork; usually used as a garnish for broth soups or served in tomato sauce as an appetizer or light entrée

Andouille: a coarse-grained smoked meat made using pork, pepper, onions, wine and seasonings

B

Balsamic vinegar: made from a reduction of cooked white Trebbiano grape juice and not a vinegar in the usual sense; highly valued by chefs and gourmet food lovers; aged a minimum of 12 years

Bisque: a thick cream soup, especially of pureed shellfish or vegetables

Braised: to cook (meat, fish or vegetables) by sautéing in fat and then simmering slowly in very little liquid

Brine: Water that is saturated with salt used for preserving meat or poultry

C

Cannelloni: tubular or rolled pieces of pasta, usually filled with a mixture of meat or poultry and cheese, then baked in a cream or tomato sauce

Capellini: a very thin variety of pasta (even thinner than vermicelli)

Caramelized onions: onion slices cooked in a little butter for a rich sweetness and slight smoky flavor

Chevre: goat cheese

Mediterranean
Capellini, 100

Chorizo sausage: a term encompassing several flavor types of pork sausage ranging from smoky to spicy/hot; usually dry cured and flavored with garlic, herbs & spices along with paprika, which gives it the characteristic red color

Chutney: a condiment containing spices, fruit & vegetables; vinegar is often added as a preservative

Clafoutis: a baked French dessert of black cherries arranged in a butter dish and covered with a thick flan-like batter; dusted with powdered sugar and served lukewarm

Confit: a French dish made with the leg of a duck by curing the meat with salt and then poaching it in its own fat

Coq au Vin: chicken stewed in a sauce of wine, diced pork, onions, garlic and mushrooms

Couscous: pellets of semolina (inner part of durum wheat) used as a side dish or in salads

Currants: a small dried seedless grape of the Mediterranean region, used in cooking

Cherry Almond
Clafoutis, 151

E

English cucumber: longer, narrower and thinner skinned than regular cucumbers; usually wrapped in plastic; unwaxed

F

Flan: (also called caramel custard) a custard dessert topped with a layer of soft caramel

Frittata: an omelet resembling a large pancake and containing vegetables, seasonings and cheeses

G

Ghee: butter clarified by boiling used in Indian cuisine

Gnocchi: thick, soft dumplings available dried, frozen or fresh; usually accompanied with tomato sauce, pesto or melted butter

H

Hominy: Hulled and dried kernels of corn, prepared by boiling

Hummus: a paste or dip made of chickpeas (garbanzo beans) mashed with oil, garlic, lemon juice and tahini usually eaten with pita bread or chips

L

Lassi: a popular yogurt-based drink of India; traditionally, yogurt is blended with water and Indian spices

Leek: a vegetable in the onion and garlic family; the edible portions are the white onion base and light green stalk; the taste is similar to a mild onion and cucumber mixture

M

Mahi Mahi: Though this is actually a type of dolphin, it shouldn't be confused with the dolphin that is a mammal. To avoid this misunderstanding, the Hawaiian name mahi mahi is becoming more widespread. Also called dolphinfish and Dorado, mahi mahi is found in warm waters throughout the world. It's a moderately fat fish with firm, flavorful flesh

Honey Rose Lassi, 165

Marinade: a seasoned liquid, usually of vinegar or wine with oil, herbs and spices in which meat, fish or vegetables are soaked before cooking

Moo Shu: A stir-fried Chinese dish containing shredded pork, scallions and various seasonings. This mixture is scrambled with eggs, rolled in small thin pancakes (called moo shu pancakes or Peking doilies) and served hot

Muddled (limes): the lime is well scrubbed, cut into eighths and placed in the base of a sturdy glass with 2 tsp. sugar; then a flat ended rolling pin is taken and strong rotating movements are used to "muddle" the lime pieces with the sugar until the fruit has exuded its fragrant juices and the skins have released their essential oils

Muscovy duck: a large duck native to Mexico, Central and South America

P

Parchment paper (baking paper): Waterproof and grease-resistant paper used in baking as a disposable non-stick surface

Phyllo: flaky, tissue thin layers of pastry used in baked desserts and appetizers

Posole: a thick, stew like soup of pork or chicken, hominy, mild chili peppers and coriander leaves; traditionally served at Christmas and often favored as a hangover remedy

Pots de Crème: (pot of custard) a loose French dessert; not as "set" as custards or flans

Prosciutto: salted ham that has been cured by drying; always sliced paper thin for serving

Pulse: Turning on & off quickly when using a blender

Puree: cooked food that has been put through a sieve (strainer) or blender to make it soft and smooth

MarketSpice Chocolate
Pots de Crème, 146

Q

Quiche: a pie-like dish consisting of an unsweetened pastry shell filled with custard containing cheese, vegetables, seafood or ham

R

Ramekin: small individual baking dishes often used for custards, soufflé's, French onion soup or a variety of other dishes

Rémoulade: a popular condiment in many countries; similar to tartar sauce but often flavored with curry; used with meats and seafood dishes such as breaded fried fish or crab cakes

Risotto: a dish of rice cooked in broth usually served with tomatoes, cheese or chicken

Roux: pronounced "roo"; a cooked mixture of wheat flour and fat used as a thickening agent for gravies, sauces, soups and stews

S

Samosas: Indian fried turnover filled with minced meat or vegetables and spices

Sangria: A Spanish drink of red wine mixed with lemonade, fruit and spices

Sauté: fry quickly in a little fat

Simmer: cooking in a liquid at or just below boiling

Soba: Japanese name for buckwheat, but in Japan refers to any thin noodle

Curried Samosas, 34

T

Tahini: a paste made from sesame seeds originating in the Middle East often used in hummus and dips

Tofu: also called bean curd; made by curdling soy milk and then pressing the resulting curds into soft white blocks; low calorie and little fat

Translucent: Clear or transparent

Trifle: A cold dessert of sponge cake and fruit covered with layers of custard, jelly and cream

Truffles: a type of chocolate confectionery, traditionally made with a chocolate ganache cream, caramel, nuts or berry center and coated with chocolate or cocoa powder

W

Wok: a large bowl-shaped pan used in Chinese cooking

Z

Zest: the grated peel or skin of an orange, lemon or lime used as flavorings in drinks or foods; often used as a garnish

Terms Glossary

Index